TREASURE LEGENDS OF THE WEST

TREASURE LEGENDS OF THE WEST

CHORAL PEPPER

GIBBS·SMITH
P
PUBLISHER

SALT LAKE CITY

DEDICATION

In memory of my father, Fred A. Carleson.

First Edition
97 96 95 94   5 4 3 2 1

Text copyright © 1994 by Choral Pepper
Artwork copyright © 1994 by Gibbs Smith, Publisher

This is a Peregrine Smith Book, published by
Gibbs Smith, Publisher
P.O. Box 667
Layton, Utah 84041

Design by Warren Archer
Artwork by Shauna Mooney Kawasaki
Lynda Sessions, Editor
Dawn V. Hadlock, Assistant Editor
Printed and bound in Hong Kong

Library of Congress Cataloging-in-Publication Data

Pepper, Choral.
Western treasure legends/Choral Pepper.
     p. cm.
ISBN 0-87905-611-8
1. Treasure-trove—West (U.S.) 2. West (U.S.)—Antiquities.
3. West (U.S.)—History, Local. 4. Legends—West (U.S.)   I. Title.
F591.P42   1994
978—dc20   94-18062
                                                 CIP

CONTENTS

ACKNOWLEDGMENTS

First I am indebted to my wonderful editor, Lynda Sessions, whose enthusiasm was as inspiring as her expertise was helpful. I am grateful that my publisher, Gibbs Smith, saw the potential in a book of this nature and determined that every page should be a "work of art." That it lived up to his expectation is the result of Shauna Mooney Kawasaki's artistic interpretations and Warren Archer's design. Madge Baird's editorial direction has also been invaluable.

Research help was forthcoming from a number of sources—especially the Coronado, California, and Salt Lake City, Utah, public libraries. Jo Ann Parker, the librarian in Crane, Texas, was generous with information in regard to her area, as was Linda Rees, the Reagan County librarian in Big Lake, Texas. My friends Joyce and Bill McKay in Montana opened doors in their area, as did Beth and Howard Summerhays of Salt Lake City, who lent us an important book.

The contributions of other friends and family members are included in the body of the book. But above all, I am appreciative of my husband Denis Thompson, who met the challenge of rugged backcountry driving which at times tested even his skill.

INTRODUCTION

No matter how far-fetched a treasure legend may sound, chances are good that it has some basis in fact. To illustrate this in modern terms, consider the case of the Hijacker's Ransom. It was on a cold, wet Thanksgiving Eve in 1971 that D. B. (Dan) Cooper bought a ticket at the Portland International airport for a flight to Seattle. Barely had the Boeing 747 nosed into the storm when Cooper threatened a stewardess with what he said was a dynamite bomb. He then demanded four parachutes and $200,000 in $20 bills. When the plane landed at Seattle, everyone but the crew and Cooper got off. The money and the parachutes that the pilot had ordered ahead by radio were delivered and, on Cooper's orders, the plane took off immediately for Reno. They were flying somewhere over southwest Washington when Cooper strapped the twenty-one pounds of money to his body and bailed out.

The following night, the FBI reenacted the skyjacking in the same plane with the same crew, fuel load, altitude, and speed. This was to aid flight engineers and meteorologists in computing Cooper's probable drop zone. It proved to be a trapezoidal area covering about twenty-five square miles. Although the area was searched repeatedly, neither Cooper nor the money—all in marked bills—surfaced until some years later when a boy accidentally dug up $5,880 worth of water-soaked bills along a bank of the Columbia River. They proved to be a small portion of the marked ransom money.

Cooper had been inadequately clothed for the chilling temperature at which he jumped, and he appeared to be inexperienced as a skydiver. It was considered doubtful that he escaped alive unless, of course, he did manage to land and had clothes and disguises stashed in advance. If not, the remainder of the $200,000 is still where it fell.

This incident is bound to provoke a treasure legend for future generations. In spite of the fact that ten thousand paper $20 bills would hardly survive southwest Washington's wet winters, when the story is told to future generations, it will still have a basis in fact.

D. B. Cooper's booty consisted of a perishable substance. The legendary lost loot from highwaymen, ancient Spanish mines, a wrecked galleon, buried coins, lost treasure caches, and rich ore ledges as recounted in this book may be as elusive as Cooper's marked bills, but they are more durable.

Treasure legends of the American West were born in the sixteenth century when the Spanish in Mexico started to develop mines as far north as Utah. Like Cooper's bills, the fortunes that their Indian slaves were forced to wrest from the earth were also marked. One-fifth of all gold and silver produced was poured into molds designated with a symbol indicating that it belonged to the King of Spain. The King's allotment, called the "Royal Fifth," was then safely stashed until a mule train transported it to a Mexican port from whence it was shipped to Spain. Tax dodging is nothing new, however. Countless isolated Spanish mines were worked illicitly, which today enrich our legendary West.

In addition to Spanish treasure troves, lost caches left by prospectors who followed in the wake of California's gold rush still taunt seekers. Often, documentation of these caches was ambiguous, consisting of nothing more than a waybill or map divulged on a deathbed. John Nummel, on the other hand, actually held the promise of fortune in his hand. Time and trails, even short ones, are deceptive when we try to recall them at the end of a long trek, especially desert trails where there are no trees to mark the way.

Of more substance than waybills were caches secreted for protection against bandits or Indian raids, such as the lost Custer payroll and Maximilian's gold. Tales of these caches, consisting of known amounts, have ended up on our television screens.

Luck plays a role in finding treasure, but there are aids to help it along. The most important aid is an understanding of the territory. Topographical maps should be studied closely. By identifying mountains, valleys, old trails, mines and springs, it is possible to sit in New York and plot the probable locations of treasures described in this book.

In developing clues, a knowledge of history and an understanding of life as it was lived at the time is also extremely important. Many of us stop right there. My own interest in running down old treasure legends lies in what I learn about a region rather than in the actual pursuit of riches. Like my pleasure in sighting a rainbow, the pot of gold is not an end in itself. I am a writer, not a professional treasure seeker, even though much of the material for this book came from personal experience.

Readers will find numerous references to the former *Desert Magazine*. It was a publication begun by Randall Henderson in the 1930s that covered the history, geology, archaeology, flora, fauna, legends, colorful characters, old trails, and anything else relating to western deserts. I purchased the magazine in 1963 and edited it until I sold it in 1970. Countless legends of lost mines and buried treasures appeared on our pages, many told for the first time and contributed by readers who culled them from early family records. During summer months, I broadened our format to include adventures into "cool country for hot desert dwellers," which brought to my attention legends of lost treasures beyond desert areas, some of which are included in this book.

Treasure legends are an integral part of Western Americana. Through them, our country's history is most provocatively told. It has been a particular pleasure for me to be able to introduce this part of our American culture to an urbane "alien"—my London-born husband Denis Thompson. We hope that others who have never experienced the excitement of a metal detector whine or been the first to spot an ancient treasure sign carved on a tree will be enticed to come out and join the fun.

Choral Pepper
Coronado, California

CUSTER'S LAST PAYROLL

From Cody, Wyoming, to Billings, Montana, every rancher with whom my husband Denis and I have ever talked has assured us that the famous lost gold consignment destined to subsidize General Custer's last payroll would someday be found in an ice cave in the Pryor Mountains. Ranchers showed us a "lost treasure" book describing Montana's most famous treasure legend which "proved" that the payroll must be buried along the old wagon trail that passed through Pryor Valley, just east of the connecting highway between the two ranching communities. The Pryor Mountains had to be the place. Right?

Wrong!

The real story behind the lost gold consignment came to light very recently, when its most likely location was revealed in a scholarly treatise that had nothing to do with lost loot. The thrust of the study was an historical account of riverboats that once plied the Little Big Horn. It was in the log of the riverboat the *Far West* that the key to the riddle and the final disposition of the lost consignment of gold was found.

While the study did not concern Custer's famous "last stand," Custer's tragedy is firmly bound to the treasure legend and so, is a good place to begin our story. Custer's "last stand" took place in Montana's valley of the Little Big Horn River on 25 June, 1876. When all was over, Custer, fourteen officers, and two-hundred-thirty-three men lay dead, their bodies stripped and mutilated conforming to Indian custom.

According to the log of the *Far West*, while Custer's battle was progressing to the north, Captain Marsh was nervously piloting the river supply boat upstream towards the Montana junction of the Big Horn and Little Big Horn rivers where he was to effect an appointed rendezvous with Custer's commanding officer, General Terry. Although aware that Indians were amassing, Captain Marsh did not realize just how serious the situation had become.

This was the first trip up the Little Big Horn that Captain Marsh had made. Apprehensive as he was, as well as unfamiliar with shoreline landmarks, he failed to identify the confluence of the two rivers, where he was to effect the rendezvous with General Terry. Promising diversions in the waterway turned out to be nothing more than deltas. A heavy growth of reeds and cottonwood trees edging the shore obscured the channel. Finally, to his consternation, he realized that he had exceeded the rendezvous point by some fifteen to twenty miles. A small clearing on shore at that point revealed a wagon road that led to the water. Marsh decided that the prudent thing would be to tie up there for the night and try to rendezvous back downstream the following morning.

At the same time, a mule-drawn freight wagon was headed in the direction of the river with a consignment of gold to supplement U.S. Army payrolls at a division center in Bismarck, North Dakota. Its driver, Gil Longworth, and his two armed guards were also aware of the rising Indian hostility.

While Captain Marsh waited at anchor, the terror-stricken wagon driver Longworth

General George Custer, hero or blunderer?
—Utah Historical Society

arrived at the crossing on his wagon and stopped to warn the captain that the entire area was swarming with militant Indians, and that he doubted his chances of living long enough to get the gold shipment delivered to Bismarck. As the two men exchanged views, it occurred to Longworth that the consignment might be safer if held aboard the boat with Marsh until it could be delivered at a calmer time. Marsh agreed and the payroll gold was transferred to the boat. A relieved Longworth turned his wagon back towards Bozeman, Montana, where his shipment had initiated.

According to the log of the *Far West,* the transfer of the gold consignment to the boat occurred on 26 June. Neither of the parties involved knew that on the previous day Custer and his troops had been slaughtered on the opposite side of the river.

As night fell, the scene on the river changed. An acrid smell permeated the air. Flames from Indian camps sprung up along the mesa on the east side of the river and Captain Marsh found his position as jeopardized as Longworth's! He discussed the volatile situation with his two trusted officers, first mate Thompson and engineer Foulk. Both agreed that the safest procedure would be to bury the gold in a suitable spot ashore until Indian unrest subsided.

Spyglass in hand, Marsh crept beyond the thick stand of trees along the riverbank. He was encouraged that no sign of Indian fires interrupted the empty plain to the south

and west, but neither did the relentlessly flat terrain suggest a suitable hiding place for the gold. As his glass swept to a northwest view, the terrain changed. A long, low ridge of eroded sandstone studded with scrubby pines interrupted the unbroken span and angled obliquely towards the river.

Hauling their precious consignment in a handcart, the three officers branched northwest from the wagon trail leading to the river and followed an animal trail towards the ridge. In the gloaming light of the June evening, dark crevices that yawned from its side promised a place to secure the cache. One of the men stumbled, almost upsetting the awkward cart. When he turned to right it, he saw a spiral of smoke curl above the horizon to the southwest. It was the first Indian signal they had seen on their side of the river. Marsh hurried them along. He had guessed that the ridge lay about a mile from shore, but now it appeared more like two miles. The sky darkened. Another spiral of fire snaked up in the west. The handcart tottered clumsily over the rough earth. Marsh began to think that, as Longworth had feared, he might not live long enough to safely dispose of the gold and keep his morning rendezvous down the river.

At last they reached the ridge. Marsh guarded the handcart while his men probed the terrain. About midway up the incline, they found an unobtrusive cave with an opening

Sioux chief Sitting Bull's reputation for bravery may have evolved from his shrewd political finesse rather than courage on the battlefield. A practicing medicine man, he usually resorted to that skill in times of danger. Whether or not he participated actively at Custer's last stand, he was chief of the hostile Indian camp and later reported that Custer was among the last to die.

Far West riverboat which plied the Big Horn and carried supplies to the troops.
−Montana Historical Society

partially blocked by a scrubby pine. It required the might of all three men to boost the heavy leather bags up to it. Marsh had had the foresight to carry a shovel and axe. Before heading back to the river, the men effectively disguised the eroded cavity with dead branches and debris. Then, dragging the empty handcart, they returned safely to their boat.

Not until forty-eight hours later, after Marsh had traveled back downstream and succeeded in making contact with General Terry's main army, did he learn about the slaughter of Custer's men on the east bank of the river and the severe losses in troops who were engaged in another skirmish to the south that had been led by Major Reno.

Gil Longworth and his guards fared no better. They had returned only as far as Pryor's Creek about fifty miles west of the river where, a day or two later, another freighter discovered their bullet-riddled bodies alongside their burned-out wagon.

Detailed now to carry Reno's casualties downriver for treatment, Captain Marsh left the area. Due to further tension between Indians and whites, it was three years before he again took a riverboat up the Big Horn and heard of Longworth's fate. By that time, the Bozeman freight company that employed him had, like its competitors, ceased

operation due to Indian raids.

Marsh, Foulk and Thompson, the only individuals aware of the hidden cache of gold, all passed the rest of their lives making an honest living working on riverboats. None of their future activities indicated in any manner that they had struck it rich.

This, of course, does not preclude the possibility that one or all three tried to find the hidden gold. This would not have been easy. The cache had been hidden in the dark of night in territory unfamiliar to them and under circumstances of intense duress. That they didn't return to the area for three years, and then only briefly on a river run, would have further complicated recovery. However, as we now know, there is an even more compelling reason to believe that the treasure remains undiscovered.

Officials in Bozeman who were responsible for the gold shipment assumed when they learned of Longworth's massacre that he and his guards had been *en route* to their destination, with the gold still in their keeping—a logical misconception since the only living persons aware of its transfer to the *Far West* had departed the area before the bodies and burned wagon were found at Pryor Creek. When no subsequent display of

unseemly wealth by local Indians developed, interested parties suspected that Longworth, apprehensive of the attack, had detoured from the wagon trail into Pryor Mountain to secrete the gold.

The log book report concerning the true disposition of the gold consignment and its transfer from Longworth's wagon to the *Far West* revealed that Captain Marsh and his two officers had completed the task of securing their charge ashore and were back aboard the boat within three-and-a-half hours. As succinct as that information may appear, when combined with a little deductive thinking and a first-hand view of the area, the hallowed old legend becomes enhanced by its change of venue.

Charlie Russell, early cowboy artist, depicts mounted Sioux Indians whom military men described as the finest cavalry men in the world.

Captain Marsh stated that he had mistakenly proceeded some fifteen to twenty miles above his intended rendezvous at the confluence of the Little Big Horn and the Big Horn rivers and had anchored at an apparent river crossing when Longworth happened along. Even today, with countless deltas interrupting the rivers' channels, the meeting place of the two rivers would be easily missed were it not for the community of Hardin, Montana, which straddles the juncture.

Denis and I drove north on State Highway 47 from the rivers' confluence at Hardin. The highway followed the river's path, but some distance west of its bank. Assuming that Captain Marsh was correct in his estimate of being fifteen miles above the intended

rendezvous point, we were excited to see a sign at about that mileage mark that read "Fishing Access." Flanked by corn fields, the dirt road led to the river's edge. We paused along the way to talk with a local farmer who assured us that it was at this commonly used old wagon crossing that General Custer had forded the river prior to making his "last stand"— a fact confirmed by a sign on the river's bank that identified the site as the "General Custer Fishing Access."

We strolled among the thick tangle of trees whose branches overhung the water. It was easy here to imagine the drama of that June night over a century ago when Indian smoke signals rising over the low, bare mesas to the east witnessed Custer's tragic defeat and caused two terrified men to speculate upon their own chances of survival.

Surveying the land west of the tree-lined bank where Marsh had anchored, we could appreciate his dilemma. No feasible hiding place suggested itself in the monotonous flat land that extended for miles. But as our eyes moved northward, a gradual rise of land angled obliquely towards the river. Now called Pine Ridge, we felt certain that this accent against the horizon was the break in the landscape that provided Marsh with a safe place to stash the consignment.

Recalling that he and his men had buried the gold and returned to the *Far West* within a period of three-and-a-half hours, Denis and I retraced our route along the dirt road back to the highway. It was exactly one mile. Figuring that Marsh's party would have covered at least two miles an hour, we drove north along the highway for a little more than another mile. At this point we were close enough to the mantle of eroded sandstone studded with scrawny pines to eliminate any doubt that Marsh could have secreted the treasure on Pine Ridge and returned to the anchorage within the prescribed time.

To all appearances, this ridge that rises above neatly plowed fields lies fallow. Until

this verified version of the lost gold consignment's disposition on Pine Ridge seeps into Montana's legendary history, treasure hunters will be fruitlessly scouring the Pryor Mountains some sixty miles to the west. Denis and I agreed—this would be some of the easiest treasure ever to recover.

A treasure so valuable and accessible; a site so unexploited—these factors added up to the treasure-hunting opportunity of the decade. And, but for the love of a cat, we would have won it first. Whoever does find this treasure will owe his good fortune to a Siamese cat named Tiggy. She was home alone, three days away. We simply hadn't the heart to delay our return to her another minute!

Pine Ridge, Montana. Hiding place for Custer's last payroll cache?

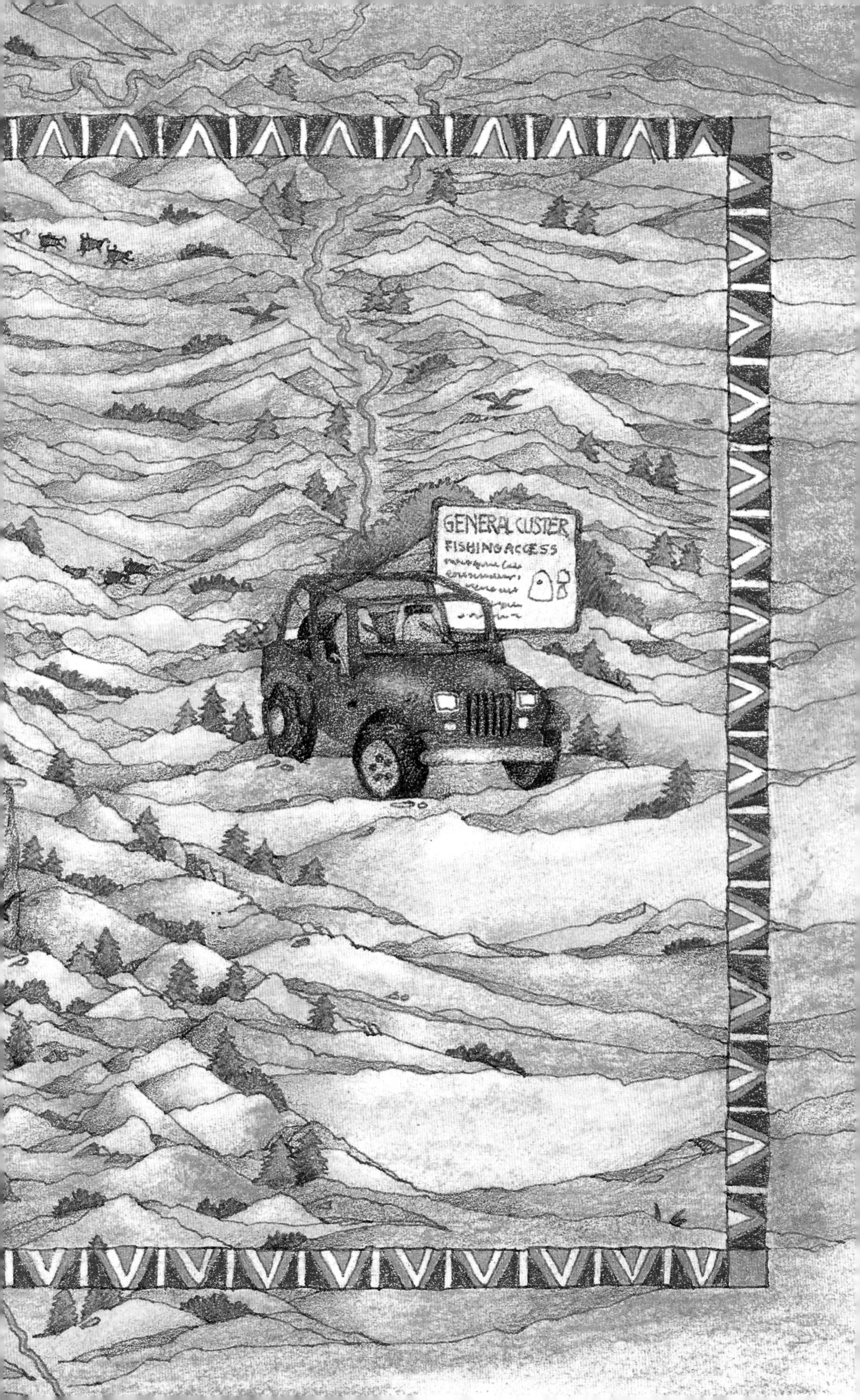
GENERAL CUSTER
FISHING ACCESS

LOOKING FOR GOLD IN ALL THE WRONG PLACES

Protecting his eyes with a camera, Trent Lowe squeezed between branches that snapped against the car. In the narrow dirt road, he focused into the heavy shadows, clicked a quick photo and ducked back into his seat.

"What's your hurry?" I asked.

"Noises," he answered sheepishly.

I opened my window and knew what he meant. Unseen wings swished in the foliage. Crackles, whines, whirs and buzzes haunted the black shadows. It wasn't like any desert ought to be. Then abruptly the willowy growth along the river came to an end and we entered into a melee of naked sunbaked hills studded with lava boulders. This was the Trigo Mountain Range on the Arizona side of the Colorado River, a sere, arroyo-gutted land responsible for bashing old John Nummel's dream of paving his streets with gold.

My young son and I were making this trip in response to a telephone call from Erle Stanley Gardner, the famed creator of "Perry Mason" detective books. During the time that I edited *Desert Magazine*, Gardner and I had shared a number of adventures in Baja California. Those adventures had always entailed months

Trent Lowe and I entered into a jungle where no jungle had any business to be.

of complicated planning and advance research, so I was surprised to hear him suggest a short, three-day trek to Arizona.

The call was inspired by a story about a man named Nummel that had appeared in the magazine long before I purchased it. Gardner figured that with metal detectors, a helicopter, and the recreational vehicles available to us today, we could find a solution to old Nummel's plight.

But first, someone had to go into the forbidding terrain to locate a campsite with a level area for the helicopter pad and a relatively accessible road. I volunteered.

Nummel's sad story began in the late 1880's when he was caretaker for the rich Red Cloud silver and lead mine on the Arizona side of the Colorado River. He lived in a cabin on his own homestead at Norton's Landing, a mining community and river port some seven miles from the mine. Each day he commuted to the mine and back to his shack by foot.

One day, in a temperamental huff resulting from harsh words with his boss, Nummel quit his job at Red Cloud Mine. This was not the first time. In spite of an erratic temper, he was a good worker and both he and the supervisor knew that eventually he would be back. A resumé of Nummel's career would have listed just about every mine in southwestern Arizona, but Red Cloud was his favorite. Initially this may have been because it was located close to his homestead. Later there was a more important reason. On this occasion, he set off at dawn to seek a new job at La Fortuna Mine, about sixty-five miles away. Some miners would have traveled by burro, but Nummel shunned the animals. You had to feed and water them. He had figured out a shortcut that roughly paralleled an old Indian trail that passed through a region filled with

shadowed arroyos (gullies) that he would follow during the hottest part of the day. A huge pothole, or natural rock basin, lay not far from his intended shortcut, so he wouldn't have to carry water.

Nummel purposefully crossed Yuma Wash in the Trigos while the sun was still low and continued on in a southeasterly direction. When he met the old Indian trail, he followed it for awhile, and then broke off into untried terrain to pursue his own contemplated shortcut. At high noon, he sank gratefully against the bank of an arroyo shaded by a big paloverde tree. There he ate a sandwich and drank the remaining water in his canteen. This would have been foolhardy with fifty-odd miles yet to walk, but Nummel calculated that the natural water tank couldn't be more than a mile distant. There had been a recent summer storm. It would be full of fresh water.

Nummel had been a prospector most of his life. Whenever he noticed an outcrop of quartz, no matter how unpromising, he chipped off a sample with his prospector's pick. He now mechanically hacked off a chunk of dirty yellow quartz from a ledge on the bank of the wash beside him.

Back in the 1880's when Nummel (second from left) arrived, this was a world of hard men with ambitious dreams—a world of millworkers, freighters, stage drivers, stable keepers, store keepers, bartenders and miners who came from everywhere. The miners, many adventure-seeking Europeans lured by German translations of Bret Harte novels, were called "ten-day" men because most of them drifted from one district to another, staying that many days. During its heyday, the colorful Bret Harte himself prospected in the Trigo silver district where millions and millions of dollars of silver, lead and zinc were taken in the 1880s.

Its reverse side was loaded with free gold, the richest ore Nummel had ever seen. When he had regained his wits, he settled down to take stock of the situation. First, he could not stay where he was because his canteen was empty. He had neither provisions to set up a camp, nor tools other than his prospector's pick. If he returned to the Red Cloud right after having quit in a huff, the other miners would deduce his strike. He had to keep it a secret until he had registered a claim. If he put up a location monument, someone might pass this way and jump his claim. The most practical solution, he decided, was to simply camouflage the ledge until he could return to work it.

After hiding the ledge with dead wood, he carefully placed his quartz sample into his knapsack and hiked to the natural water tank—an important clue when Nummel stated later that he had made his strike within a mile of it.

After filling his canteen, Nummel continued on to La Fortuna, southeast of Yuma. There he succeeded in getting a job because of his reputation as a competent worker. This time, however, he proved to be unusually ambitious. Now he was intent upon earning enough money to develop his secret gold strike so he could spend the rest of his life in luxury.

When at last his savings were adequate, he precipitated an argument with the boss as an excuse to quit his job, and caught a ride on a wagon going north. The route carried him closer to Norton's Landing on the Colorado than to the scene of his strike, so he went first to his homestead, intending to get supplies before heading back for a more thorough inspection of his potential mine.

Back home again with money in his pocket and the promise of a rich future, Nummel jubilantly waived his new ban against booze and joined old friends at the saloon. When he sobered up a day or two later, his money was spent.

Ruins from World War II structures contrasted grimly with those of the 1880's. Red Cloud had died twice—once in 1890; then it was revived to die again in 1949 when the price of silver dropped too low to make mining profitable. The flimsily built latter structures resembled temporary film sets, but the substantial remains of the older foundations suggested faith in an everlasting bonanza.

"TEN-DAY" MEN

Nummel went back to work at Red Cloud, this time remaining sober through enough paychecks to purchase some primitive mining equipment. At last he set forth to open his mine.

He retraced his steps through Yuma Wash and along the old Indian trail from which he had branched off for his shortcut, but finding his gold ledge again was not that easy. Each time he struck out in a direct southeasterly direction, he wound up in a different place. This proved to him that the untrod path he had chosen when he found his strike could have fallen anywhere within a wide range of empty desert.

His only dependable landmark was the pothole. From it Nummel circled in ever widening spirals, like ripples in a pond of sand. Shallow arroyos fanned out in patterns as complicated as a spider web. Paloverde trees, with their deep roots sucking up moisture after desert storms, flourished along the banks of most of them, but none seemed to shade a camouflaged ledge studded with gold.

John Nummel never gave up. When too old to risk the long hikes, he confided his secret to a younger miner who eventually inherited the elusive gold-laced quartz and pursued a fruitless life-long search of his own. Today, it is still lost, but perhaps as a result of the Gardner expedition, a little less lost.

As the advance party of the Gardner expedition, my son and I, after breaking out of the jungle along the Colorado River north of Yuma, followed a dirt road that crossed Yuma Wash and continued to Red Cloud Mine, where Nummel had worked. An abandoned building that sagged on the riverbank west of Red Cloud bore the name Norton's Landing, but that wasn't its original location. This important dock on the Colorado was located considerably to the south during the Trigo district's heyday when Nummel lived nearby.

Gardner found Nummel's waterhole, the main clue to the location of the lost gold ledge. Probing with a walking stick into its sandy bottom proved it the deepest pothole any of us had ever found on the desert. Now we could understand why Nummel hadn't hesitated to empty his canteen before reaching it.

After scouting the area, Trent set up an overnight camp and I put our Dutch oven on charcoal. The following morning we located a campsite for Gardner and headed back to my air-conditioned office in Palm Desert, California.

It was a cool October day a month later when I returned to the Trigos with Erle Stanley Gardner, his party of explorers, and his fleet of four-wheel-drive vehicles and custom sand-buggies. Our use of the Fairchild-Hiller helicopter due to land at camp the next morning was limited to its day of arrival plus a few hours the following day. With no time to waste, we split into teams. While one set up camp, others of us explored by land to facilitate the air search. Then, as customary in Gardner camps, at day's end everyone gathered around a loin of beef crackling over the campfire to trade information.

Each had succeeded in finding a possible clue and a likely "hot spot," but when the helicopter arrived the following day and we alternated air time, not one of us could relocate our "hot spot." It is astonishing how different terrain appears from the air. Old trails are revealed that might go unnoticed on the ground even while you walk on them. Our sympathy for poor Nummel wandering aimlessly through the maze of arroyos was enhanced. We hovered over some intriguing old mines in the helicopter and landed once to examine an outcrop, but none of the trails we located followed in the direction old Nummel had taken.

While the rest of us lolled around the campfire lamenting our failure, Doug Allen, a cinematographer who had arrived with the helicopter crew, borrowed my

topographical map and withdrew to the light of an oil lamp. Later we learned that Doug had graduated from Stanford University with a degree in geography and once had made a study of tracing ancient Indian paths.

At dawn, with barely an hour left before the helicopter had to take off for San Diego, Gardner shouted orders. "You guys break camp. We'll take a look." The chopper was already winging up dust. We raced to the contrived landing pad, ducking as we ran to avoid its propellers.

Because hikers generally overestimate mileage, Doug instructed the pilot to hover somewhat short of three miles up Yuma Wash where Nummel thought he had crossed to follow the old Indian trail. Doug was right. A clear, firm Indian trail cut in a southeasterly direction through the rough terrain. According to Nummel's report, he had varied from this trail to make his own, but Doug doubted that he had wandered very far afield due to the particular lay of the land for walking.

J. W. Black and Gardner explore in one of the custom-built vehicles Black had manufactured when Gardner requested a light-weight, maneuverable vehicle that wouldn't tear up the desert. Built with a VW engine and individual wheel suspension, it floated, climbed and crawled over the roughest of terrain, a great aid to desert exploration when time was limited.

By this time we had flown beyond the Trigo Range and were advancing into the Chocolate Mountains, a low twenty-five-mile-long range that lies between the Trigos and Nummel's destination at La Fortuna Mine. There was no trail to follow now. Maybe Nummel had strayed further than Doug thought. We instructed the pilot to land and then we set out on foot.

Paloverde trees grew all over the place, so we ignored them as a clue. To save time, we fanned out, each looking for the pothole.

Gardner was the one to find it. With a shout that would put a coyote's yip to shame, he brought Doug and me on the run to see the deepest most perfectly formed natural rock basin we had seen in any desert country—certainly one that would have held water following a good storm for a matter of months. Several feet of sand had blown into the lower part, disguising its true depth until Gardner poked his walking stick down to the bottom.

While J. W. Black studies a topographical map, Gardner dispatches each team in a different direction to search for clues to Nummel's lost ledge.

It appeared to us now that Nummel's gold ledge was lost in the Chocolate Mountains, rather than in the adjacent Trigos where legend had established it. Not only was the pothole here, but geological evidence lent credence to the Chocolates as the site of Nummel's gold. For this range lies only a few miles north of the rich Laguna placers, an area of potholes filled with placer (surface) grains of gold that were found by construction workers who impounded the Colorado River to build Laguna Dam in 1907. The gold, having eroded from a mother vein far inland from the river's present shore, had been carried down by flash floods and deposited in cliff-side potholes sometimes a hundred feet above the water.

"Let me see that topo map again." Gardner shoved his hat to the back of his head and studied the map. "Now it looks to me," he observed in true Perry Mason fashion, "that if anything like a straight line were possible in this arroyo-gutted land, Nummel could have walked almost directly east from his homestead at Norton's Landing before turning south to reach La Fortuna and his trail would have passed near where we stand now. But," he paused for emphasis, "*if* he had headed out from the Red Cloud Mine immediately upon quitting his job, he would have followed Yuma Wash directly south, thus avoiding the Chocolates, and he would not have met up with this pothole."

Gardner squinted into the horizon, mentally putting himself in the old miner's shoes. "We know from Nummel's own account," he continued, "that he started out

early in the morning to avoid heat. Now, wouldn't a guy as desert-savvy as old Nummel go home after quitting his job to catch a good night's sleep before starting out on that long walk—especially when the route from his homestead was shorter than from where he worked?"

Like others before us, had we been looking for gold in all the wrong places? Did Nummel deliberately mislead those he told about his find by letting them assume his trail to La Fortuna initiated at Red Cloud after he had quit his job instead of at his homestead; or had his booze-befogged mind simply forgotten? One thing he was right about, though, was the deep pothole. So far as is known, ours is the only party, except for Nummel, to have succeeded in relocating it.

Regrettably, before "Perry Mason" could solve "The Case of Nummel's Lost Gold," Gardner had to return to his Temecula, California, ranch to approve a new television script. I had a magazine to get out. The rest of the crew had jobs to keep. We intended to redeem old Nummel's faith at a later date, but never made it. Now Gardner, who died in 1970, never will. But someday, someone will. And when that someone finds Nummel's gold-laden ledge, it will lie about a mile from the pothole in the Chocolates. You can bet on it!

Old trails that you might expect to find at a given point aren't always there, which was the result in our case. Where Gardner was certain that we would find the old Indian trail Nummel had followed for a short distance, no trail whatsoever marked the land. Unlike old soldiers, desert trails don't "just fade away."

THE TRINIDAD TREASURE

The year was 1927. Dr. Joseph Markey sat in his Oceanside, California, office examining an "old Indian" skull that a farmer had dug up in nearby San Luis Rey Valley. Although by profession an ophthalmologist, Markey's avocation, archaeology, often took precedence. Three years earlier he had participated in the China dig that produced Peking Man. In subsequent years he was to direct archaeological expeditions in Java, Germany, France, England, Morocco and Tahiti. His expertise was such that unusual findings, like the skull he now examined, were brought to him all of the time. And indeed this particular skull was unusual, considering the site at which it was found.

The skull was toothless, and there were no roots to the teeth in the jaw, suggesting scurvy. Dental problems of this nature were not common to early Indians. Markey sent the skull to the University of California at Los Angeles. His suspicions were confirmed. The skull was about four hundred years old and once had been attached to the body of a European white man who probably died of scurvy.

The date perplexed Markey. Scurvy was a dietary disease common

Dr. J. J. Markey examining the skulls of Ulloa crew members which he discovered in a San Luis Rey Valley cave.

28

to early sailors, but four hundred years earlier was 1527, fifteen years prior to Cabrillo's celebrated landing which is marked by a monument on San Diego's Point Loma. Traditionally, California has honored Juan Rodriquez Cabrillo, the great Portuguese navigator, as the first white man to set foot in the state. Was it possible that California's

discoverer was not Cabrillo after all? Was the state paying homage to the wrong man?

Markey accompanied the farmer to the site where he found the skull. It lay in an inviting place which had once been a lake bank lapped gently by water. With the help of local Indians, Markey and the farmer unearthed a piece of Spanish leathered armor, a rusty knife, and bits of metal that also dated back four hundred years. The only plausible explanation Markey could imagine was that the skull belonged to one of Cabrillo's sailors. However, then, as now, sailors who died at sea were buried at sea and Cabrillo was not known to have put ashore near the San Luis Rey River.

Thus began a quest that covered two continents, continued for thirty years, cost Markey over $100,000, and led to a discovery that thoroughly convinced him that another Spanish explorer, Francisco de Ulloa, was California's true discoverer. Markey did recover a small portion of the ten-million-dollar treasure that accompanied Ulloa's fourteenth-century expedition, but the major portion still rests off Oceanside's shore in the hold of the Spanish explorer's caravel, the *Trinidad*.

Ulloa's adventure began on July 8, 1539, when Hernan Cortez, the discoverer of Mexico, sent him north from Acapulco to search for the fabled "Seven Golden Cities of Cibola." Subsidized with $10,000,000 in gold and coins, Ulloa's fleet of three caravels was diminished by one during a fracas with adversaries in the Gulf of California. Upon discovering that there was no access to the Pacific through the Baja Peninsula, Ulloa sailed back down the gulf to round the cape, finally landing at Cedros Island off the Pacific Coast of Baja California.

There, a devious plot began to fester. Why should Cortez get all the glory when Ulloa took all the risks? He would send the *Aqueda*, his accompanying vessel, back to Acapulco

The cluster of boulders engraved with Indian petroglyphs which identified the site of Ulloa's burial place. (Archaeologists today frown upon chalking petroglyphs.)

and continue on to Cibola with the *Trinidad*. Then, laden with the golden city's treasures, he would sail on to Spain and reap royal patronage and wealth for himself!

According to the *Aqueda's* log, upon the ship's safe return to Mexico, Ulloa removed the money chest to the smaller *Trinidad* and then, accompanied by a scribe named Pablo Salvador Hernandez, a crew of twenty-three men, and five of the fleet's prostitutes, sent the *Aqueda* on its way back to Mexico and sailed northward on the single ship.

Nothing more was known of Ulloa's fate until Dr. Markey happened to meet a Spanish aristocrat named Miguel de Ulloa at a dinner party in Paris in 1951, some four hundred years later. Commenting that he had done considerable research on the explorer Francisco de Ulloa, Markey was elated to find that his new acquaintance was a direct descendant.

"Where did he die?" Markey asked casually.

The young man shrugged. He knew that his ancestor had perished on the same voyage along with all but one of his crew and a scribe because of a story handed down in his family of an incredible two-thousand-mile journey the two survivors had made from somewhere in Alta California to Acapulco. He knew no further details, but thought that there must be a record of the survivors' journey in Spain's Naval archives in Seville.

Within days Markey was in Seville where he hired three professional researchers with the necessary credentials to comb Naval files in search of Hernandez's manuscript. After working steadily for seven weeks—long expensive weeks for Markey—the scholars' results far exceeded expectations. They had found the original report made by the scribe to the commanding officer of the Spanish Navy upon his return to Acapulco. It was an incredible story.

It detailed how, shortly after heading north from Cedros Island, the scribe learned of Ulloa's devious plan to dupe Cortez and gain the riches of Cibola for himself. It described how this pursuit led them further and further up the West Coast where they passed the great natural harbor of San Diego, California, but since it was fed by no river, as Cibola was reputed to be, they continued on for another ten leagues. There they paused at the mouth of the San Luis Rey River to fill the ship's casks, but the river did not appear navigable so they sailed onward to the Channel Islands. At that point, Ulloa decided they were too far north for Cibola. With the women and a number of the

*O*n September 28, 1542, the Portuguese navigator Juan Rodriquez Cabrillo entered San Diego Bay with his two small caravels, San Salvador *and* Capitana, *flying the colors of the Spanish Crown. The* San Salvador, *model for the adjacent replica, is believed to have been about one hundred tons, considerably larger than the thirty-ton* Trinidad, *captained by Ulloa. After putting in at San Diego, Cabrillo visited Catalina and the Channel Islands as he progressed northward to Monterey Bay,* but made no attempt to land along the California coast between San Diego and Santa Barbara, thus establishing Ulloa, who came ashore at San Luis Rey Valley in 1539, as the earliest European to set foot in California.

Cabrillo died of injuries from a fall which occurred on San Miguel, one of the Channel Islands, when he stopped there on his return voyage in 1543. Ulloa died on a hillside in San Luis Rey Valley within months of his landfall in southern California.

crew ill from dysentery, he turned back to the river where they had replenished their water supply and anchored near its mouth.

Once anchored, Ulloa ordered the scribe Hernandez and two crew members to remain onboard ship. He then opened the money casket, filled some large leather pouches with coins to provide wages for the crew, and led a landing party ashore to a temporary camp.

When the scribe Hernandez came ashore to visit, he found about five hundred friendly Indians using the lake as both water supply and cesspool. Neither he nor a crew member with him drank the water, preferring to slake their thirst with wine, of which the ship carried plenty. This precaution saved their lives.

Does the Cabrillo Monument on San Diego's Point Loma dedicated to the "discoverer of California" honor the wrong guy? Dr. J. J. Markey believes it does.

Ulloa's camp was set up on August 21, 1540. Two days later three crew members died. On the third day, Ulloa became ill with the malignant dysentery. Others died on succeeding days. By August 31, Ulloa and the few survivors dragged themselves up a gently sloping hill on the north side of the lake, thinking they might escape death by moving away from the Indians. In the vicinity of a cluster of large boulders marked with Indian petroglyphs, they established a new camp.

Hernandez and the crew member who also drank only wine spent most of their time maintaining watch on the *Trinidad*, but every other day the scribe went ashore to confer with the captain. On one of those visits Ulloa ordered him to bury the pouches of coins about two leagues distant from camp to elude the curiosity of watchful Indians. Hernandez obeyed. He then identified it on a map which he gave to Ulloa.

The next day a heavy storm struck. For three days Hernandez did not leave ship. On the fourth day, he and a companion went to the camp. Ulloa and the last six members of the crew were dead. He dragged Ulloa's body from the cave and, after retrieving the map, buried the conquistador on the side of the hill. The other bodies he left inside the cave and covered its entrance with rocks.

The two men then returned to the *Trinidad*. The third man was ill and the ship too large to be sailed by a crew of two, so their only chance for survival was to reach civilization in the *Trinidad's* longboat. No further reference was made to the casket of treasure that Ulloa had transferred earlier from the *Santa Aqueda* to the *Trinidad*. Along with provisions there would have been no room for it in the longboat. Presumably, they left it aboard.

What could have been the most dramatic account of the scribe's report was related in the barest of detail. The third man died at sea, so the two survivors *rowed* a distance of approximately two thousand miles down the coast of Alta and Baja California and then across open sea to Acapulco!

Back home in Oceanside, with Hernandez's translated manuscript and a copy of the map citing the location of the buried coins, Markey enlisted the help of the San Luis Rey Historical Society. Recalling some boulders bearing ancient petroglyphs which another farmer had called to his attention twenty-five years earlier, Markey launched his exploration from there.

It took his party three days to find the cave shelter with its entrance buried under a heavy growth of scrub oak. Easing himself into the small cavern, he found on its floor seven skeletons—six male and one female.

Locating the coins took longer. The lake had shrunk to the size of a reed-filled

pond and the terrain had changed. Two leagues equaled approximately six miles, but there was always a question as to how conscientiously Hernandez had followed Ulloa's orders. Markey searched for six years. Finally, on a cool day in September of 1957, his metal detector buzzed at a point a little more than seven miles distant from the burial cave.

Two thousand coins lay close to the surface inside the rotted remnants of leather bags. Dating from A.D. 1500 back to the Roman Empire of the first century, collectors valued them at more than $250,000. One coin alone weighed over a pound.

However, the treasure most important to Markey had yet to be found—irrevocable evidence that the *Trinidad* had put into Oceanside before Juan Rodriques Cabrillo set foot on Point Loma in 1542. And that evidence lay under the sea.

One day in the '70s I received a phone call from Markey. We had first met when I interviewed him for a chapter in *The Mysterious West*, one of my early books. Later we worked together on a television documentary. His investigation of Ulloa's voyage had intrigued me, so when a yachtsman offered him the use of a boat and crew for a day to search for the *Trinidad*, I was invited.

Around that same time another friend of mine, the Australian electronics wizard whose motion detector had saved American soldiers' lives during guerrilla warfare in Viet Nam, was developing an underwater detector. It occurred to me that introducing the two men might be of mutual benefit. Bill Osborne could give his experimental model a trial run and if it uncovered the *Trinidad*, Markey's dedication to proving Ulloa the true discoverer of California would be realized.

So, the three of us, accompanied by a pair of experienced scuba divers, boarded the borrowed yacht. Because our use of it was limited to only a few hours, we had no time to waste. Logically, the *Trinidad* would have been held at anchor close to shore,

so we set the yacht adrift with Oceanside's low profile still in full view.

Water lapped lazily against the boat's stern while Markey and Osborne hung over the rail anxiously watching for bubbles to indicate the divers' ascension. In less than an hour they appeared, empty handed.

We sailed on to another spot, closer to where the San Luis Rey dumps into the ocean. Again our efforts were wasted. The divers were tired and came aboard for a rest. Markey's face reflected disappointment. Osborne huddled in a deck chair, biting his nails. I regretted having gotten him into it, especially considering that in those days of the "cold war" his underwater detector carried a "Secret" classification and I couldn't write the story even if we found the sunken caravel.

Giving it one more try, the divers went down for a third time. With his hands clutching the rail so hard they matched it in whiteness, Osborne's voice crackled with excitement. "They've got something!" he yelled. Indeed they had found something. It wasn't enough to claim the $10,000 prize promised by the San Luis Rey Historical Society to the finders of the *Trinidad*, but four ancient doubloons held in the diver's hand proved them on the right track. Sunken galleons off California's coasts to the north and south of

Mission San Luis Rey was founded in 1798, almost three hundred years after Ulloa was buried in San Luis Rey Valley not far from the mission.

Divers searching for the Trinidad *off the coast of Oceanside, California, examine four ancient Spanish doubloons that may provide a clue to the location of the sunken ship.*

Oceanside are a matter of record, but only Ulloa's *Trinidad* went down in waters directly off its coast. Popping champagne corks reflected Markey's elation over the four Spanish doubloons clutched in his hand.

Had this happened a decade or so earlier, Dr. Markey would have launched an ambitious underwater expedition just for the hell of it. But at this time, in his late seventies, confirmation that Ulloa got to California first as proven by the coins in his hand was satisfaction enough. For those coins exactly matched some of the ones he had recovered from Ulloa's cache buried ashore—far too improbable a circumstance to be coincidental.

Before Dr. Markey's death in the late 1980s, he was awarded the Valley Forge Medal of Honor by the Freedoms Foundation at Valley Forge, Pennsylvania, for his Ulloa research, even though the indisputable evidence of Ulloa's landing at San Luis Rey still remains buried in Pacific sands.

Just prior to publication of this book I learned of additional doubloons found following a recent storm by a girl scuba diver near Oceanside. If the scribe Hernandez was right, as he was about everything else, millions more lie down there—so close, so very very close to shore.

CUSTER'S
LAST PAYROLL

CUSTER

PINE RIDGE

PRYOR CREEK

HARDIN

LITTLE BIGHORN R.

PRYOR MOUNTAINS

THE LOST DUTCHMAN— FACT OR FANCY

Jacob Walz came to California in the 1860s to search for gold. A Heidelberg-educated German engineer whose real name was von Walzer, he posed as a Dutchman for reasons known only to himself. When California failed to endow him with riches, he wandered on to Wickenburg, Arizona.

There, in spite of his educational background, he took a job as an ordinary miner in the Vulture Gold Mine. Whether he had met the comely Apache girl named Ken-tee who also worked at the mine before he applied or afterward is uncertain, but chances are it was before. Although nearing sixty, the physically powerful, white-bearded man enchanted the young Ken-tee. Soon she became his mistress and was helping him high-grade (steal choice pieces of ore) from the mine. Suspected, an inquiry was held. Their living quarters were searched. The gold didn't turn up, but he was dismissed anyway.

Cynical "lost mine buffs" doubt that the Dutchman really had a mine. They think the gold he occasionally produced came from a hidden cache that he and Ken-tee had highgraded from the Vulture.

Others disagree. To consider their theory, we have to go back into the history of an Arizona mountain range called the Superstitions. Long before the legendary Dutchman lost his mine, the range had received its name from the Spanish explorer Coronado. The old Dutchman himself could not have chosen a

more portentous name to fit the scene of his future activities. For not only is its golden heart the home of the Apache Thunder God where storms are born, it also harbors evil spirits that pay fatal calls upon those whose footfalls attempt a trail to its treasure. Rattlesnakes, crumbling cliff edges, hundred-degree temperatures in summer, below zero in winter, random gunshots, and beheadings are only a few of the Thunder God's lethal weapons.

Francisco Vasquez de Coronado challenged the volcanic range when he came north from Mexico in 1540 to find the legendary Seven Golden Cities of Cibola. Several members of his small band succumbed in the stormy sea of grey pumice that capped its peaks. Like victims right up to recent years, their bodies later were found by companions, headless. Coronado, understandably, hastened on northward to discover the Grand Canyon.

Deterred by Apache determination to protect their sacred lands by violence if necessary, the Spaniards then left the Thunder God in peace until 1845, two centuries later, when Miguel Peralta, who had exhausted his silver mines in Mexico, arrived to claim a land grant which included the Superstitions. He came looking for silver. What he found was infinitely more precious—a vein of almost pure gold. In order to recognize the site when he returned with men and equipment, he called the hat-shaped peak that rose above his mine *Sombrero*. Later it became known as "Weaver's Needle."

Apaches sullenly watched Peralta rape their sacred land of millions of pesos' worth of pure gold concentrate which he sent to Sonora. It wasn't the gold they resented. It was the desecration of their Thunder God's home. Nor did they welcome the kidnappings and enslavement of their young people to provide labor for those mines—a resentment

Memorial to the Dutchman erected by the Dons, a distinguished organization of equestrians who make annual pack trips into the Superstitions.

38

Superstition Mountain, no place for the timid.

shared by neighboring tribes. Chief Mangas Coloradas (Red Sleeves) of the Mimbres Apaches remembered barely escaping alive when a party of white trappers in New Mexico invited his tribe to a fiesta and then massacred them to procure scalps for bounty. Chiricahua Chief Cochise, another neighbor, had been summoned to a peace conference with the white flag of truce flying over the tent. Only by intervention of his Mountain Spirit had he managed to escape alive after three bullets passed through his body.

It is little wonder that in 1848 those neighboring tribes responded to an Apache war cry to help rid the Thunder God's home of interlopers. Peralta, alerted by a Mexican worker courting an Apache girl, barely had time to remove his men and livestock to a high camp, secure the mine and disguise its entrances. His pack trains loaded the extracted gold and headed back to Mexico to await a calmer time, but it wasn't soon enough.

Apaches sprung upon the pack train's descent from the mountain's northwest end. Arrows teemed the air like migrating swallows. Stone hatchets brought down unarmed men. Pack animals bolted. Slaughter continued to the last white man on what is now known as Massacre Ground. Only Apaches lived to remember the location of the mine, but the ground where bodies later were found is a Superstition Mountain landmark.

As tragic as it was, the massacre created a legend that has enticed treasure seekers ever since. Burros fleeing into ravines and washes with gold concentrate packed heavily in their saddles were not pursued by the Indians. Even when caught for food, their captors threw aside the saddlebags as Apaches of that time had no interest in gold.

Two prospectors in the 1850s came upon three dead burros with full packsaddles. Unlike later arrivals in the Superstitions, they avoided returning to the supply town of Apache Junction where the news might have earned them a bullet. Instead, Hurley and O'Connor pounded the concentrate and panned out gold on the spot before quietly heading to the United States mint in San Francisco to collect their $37,000. From then until 1914, when the last find was reported, packsaddles stuffed with gold occasionally augmented the coffers of other roaming prospectors.

Had not the Superstition's mystique been established so dramatically and ominously by Peralta's history, one wonders if the Dutchman would have been drawn into its mysterious embrace. For after lack of evidence freed him from accusations of highgrading ore at the Vulture Mine, the white-bearded old man retired with Ken-tee to a small settlement near the mountain's foot. There the couple attracted little attention

Riders and hikers may explore the Superstitions, but no vehicles are permitted, nor is mining or the removal of artifacts.

until, following an unaccountable disappearance from home for several weeks, they returned from the mountain with two heavily laden burros. Word then escaped that Walz was making arrangements to dispatch gold to the mint in San Francisco. In gold-hungry country, that was enough to launch a legend.

Some speculated that the "Old Dutchman" had found a Peralta packsaddle. Others, especially Ken-tee's Apache relatives, had a different idea. Unaware of her possible involvement in the Vulture Mine affair, they were convinced that she had betrayed the site of the Peralta Mine, a secret closely guarded by Apaches to prevent further invasion of their sacred ground. They raided Walz's home and seized Ken-tee. Neighbors rescued her, but not before the braves had cut out her tongue. She died within an hour.

Embittered, the friendless Walz then moved to Phoenix. As far as any Walz-watchers could determine, the Old Dutchman had no interest in staking a legal claim to his mine, wherever it was. Except for intervals of heavy drinking and brawling, he lived a reclusive life in spite of avaricious gold-seekers tracking his every move. Thus they were astonished some three years later when the loner was joined by another German, a carpenter named Jacob Weiser, or Wisner.

Most believed him to be a former acquaintance. Even more astonishing was the pair's ability to elude followers when they stole away in the dark of night on a foray into the Superstitions.

Within a month, Walz and Wisner returned with sacks full of gold concentrate which they consigned to Wells Fargo for dispatch to the mint. They then set off into the Superstitions again.

This time they were less fortunate. Apaches attacked their overnight camp. Walz escaped wearing only his shirt, shoes and stockings. Wisner was found later spread-eagled over the campfire, like a piece of meat on a spit. In spite of the method, which suggested an Apache attack, many believed that Walz ruthlessly murdered his partner. It is said that he confessed to this on his deathbed.

Walz's last journey to the Superstitions produced $15,000 in gold, his legacy to a kind black woman named Julia Thomas who befriended him at the end of his life. His absence on that trip covered too short a time period for him to have mined the gold. Thus it was assumed he retrieved it from a cache. Along with the gift, he left directions to the mine for Julia to share with their few mutual friends.

The mine, he said, was in country "so rough that you could be right in the mine without seeing it." It was shaped like a funnel with the broad end uppermost and shelves cut along the wall to ease the work of bringing up ore. The mine contained an eighteen-inch vein of rose quartz studded with gold nuggets and another vein of hematite quartz about one-third gold.

"The mine is near a hideout cave," Walz further revealed. "One mile from the cave, there is a rock with a natural face looking east. To the south is Weaver's Needle. Follow to the right of the canyons, but not far. The mine faces west."

Julia Thomas and her friends spent the rest of their lives and fortunes in a fruitless search. She died in poverty after passing on her information to Jim Bark, an Arizona rancher whose fifteen-year search also produced nothing. Whether the canny Walz's directions were misleading, only he knew. What his information did suggest was that he believed the mine that produced his gold to be one and the same as Peralta's.

Gold-hungry adventurers have been searching for the Peralta Mine for years. The puzzling plight of Adolph Ruth is most notable. This elderly gentleman set forth into

the Superstitions in 1931 with a map he believed stemmed from the early Peralta family in Mexico. Ruth never came out. Six months later a rescue party found his skull, through which two bullets had been shot, close to his first camp near the floor of West Boulder Canyon. A month later, Ruth's body and possessions were recovered a considerable distance away.

Weaver's Needle, landmark for the famed Peralta Mine as well as the Dutchman's.

The map was missing. Although it appeared as an Apache-style decapitation, the theft of the map led investigators to believe otherwise.

In a pocket of Ruth's jacket was found a little book that made his the most notable of the thirty-six fatal accidents or murders that have occurred in the Superstitions. Ruth had copied instructions from the map into a notebook. He indicated that the search area was within a circle of not more than a five-mile diameter that centered on Weaver's Needle. Below the instructions, he had written the words, "*Veni, Vidi, Vici.*"

It is doubtful that the old, frail man could have covered enough of the rough terrain on his first day out to have found the mine, but those magic words were enough to set off another gold rush which resulted in the usual rash of disappearances and murders chalked up to the vengeful Thunder God.

The most recent entree to the challenge is Glenn Magill. A private investigator from Oklahoma City, he broke the code of a purported original Peralta map, from the same

A bogus "Lost Dutchman Mine" map, one of many that have circulated around Arizona since Walz's death in 1892.

source as that of the ill-fated Ruth, by inadvertently discovering that it was a mirror image of actual landmarks in the Superstitions. In 1964, Magill and the five men he enlisted in his search for the Lost Dutchman Mine initiated the most exhaustive and sophisticated quest ever undertaken. Shot at, threatened by Apaches and rattlesnakes,

tricked by swindlers, lied to, warned in letters, sabotaged, and felled by accidents, they persevered until 1967. The team uncovered a pit above a tunnel and other signs that fit Walz's clues, but no gold.

Today's most popular theory is that the hoard Ken-tee and Walz spirited away from the Venture Gold Mine was the foundation for his fortune and no real mine ever existed. If so, the crafty Walz chose a fitting site in which to bury his ill-gotten gains, with the ominous name of the mountain range itself playing into his hands.

The mysterious Superstitions lure hundreds of hikers and horseback riders to its craggy peaks annually, but the incentive for prospectors has diminished. On December 31, 1983, all National Forest Wilderness Areas, including the Superstitions, were withheld from mineral exploitation. So long as those laws are in effect, the Lost Dutchman Mine may as well remain lost.

So where is the Peralta Mine so incontrovertibly identified with the Lost Dutchman? Evidence exists that it lies considerably west of Weaver's Needle. A mine there in the Goldfield section of Superstition Range produced $3 million of gold for Denverite Charles Hall and gave birth to the once-boisterous town of Goldfield. But again, the Apache's old Thunder God issued a lusty protest. Mountains shook. Torrents of water hurtled through ravines. Everything was buried under thousands of tons of rock and sand, including the mine.

In the late 1940s, Alfred Strong Lewis, a Goldfield prospector, came upon some mysterious signs cut into the base of a large boulder. Curious, he toppled the boulder with dynamite and underneath discovered an ancient mine shaft expertly timbered in Spanish fashion with axe-cut ironwood. He climbed to a depth of seventy-five feet and found a lode of very rich ore.

Lewis proceeded to acquire partners. They had removed about $42,000 worth of gold when they broke into a larger and more modern shaft, now believed to have been part of the buried Hall shaft. If this were the Peralta Mine, the early Spaniard must have marked the rich mountain site with the boulder at the time he obliterated the shaft. Unfortunately, the vein followed by Lewis and his partners came to an end. They were forced to conclude that the mother lode had been swept away by the flood and may now lie many miles distant.

BRIGHAM'S BONANZA

When my old grandfather Edward Carleson prospected his gold mines, he wisely chose areas like Searchlight, Nevada, where every thorn of cacti stood out loud and clear. Here in Utah's pine-studded Uintas, while in search of a secret gold mine, Denis and I were pushing through undergrowth that rent our flesh and threatened every step with snake bite. I wondered if those early Mormons who followed Brigham Young from Illinois to Utah in 1846 realized how lucky they were that he directed his flock to tend to the farm and leave the mining to Cousin Jack (a colloquial term for Cornish miners, mostly Catholic, who developed Utah's mining industry).

In spite of counseling his followers that they couldn't eat gold, Brigham was aware that he couldn't build a temple and conduct business with the gentiles (non-Mormons) en route to California's goldfields without it. Prior to the gold rush, commerce had been conducted strictly by barter. With no established medium of exchange, some type of monetary system was desperately needed, yet Brigham had pledged that no gold-greedy, earth-scrounging mining activity was going to pollute his haven of Latter-day Saints. So when, in July of 1852, newly converted Chief Wakara, a friendly Ute Brigham had adopted as a son, hinted that he knew

where great quantities of gold lay just for the picking, Brigham Young believed the Mormon's money problem was solved and the legend of the Lost Mormon Mine was born.

The condition on which Wakara offered to reveal the tribal secret was that only one man besides Brigham would be apprised of an old Spanish gold cache known to the Utes, and that he would recover only enough gold for Church use.

While seeking a safe haven for persecuted worshipers following the assassination of Mormon church founder Joseph Smith, Brigham Young had sent ahead a scouting party of volunteers to acquire land in California. James Marshall, one of this party, found gold there near Sutter's Mill, thus igniting the gold rush to the West. Among those volunteers was Thomas Rhoades. Hardly had he settled his family in California when Brigham recalled the volunteers to Utah. Some ignored the summons, but Rhoades loyally answered the call, bringing with him a barrel of gold which he presented to Brigham. Rhoades's previous display of loyalty made him Brigham's choice to be the man trusted with the location of the new "Mormon Mine."

Changes that soon ensued did not go unnoticed. Rhoades built the finest house in the Salt Lake Valley and proceeded to accumulate eight wives, who in time produced

at least thirty-two children. The Mormon practice of polygamy condoned only the number of plural wives a man could support. Few men boasted of more than eight.

Not only were advances in Rhoades's fortune noted, but there was an emergence of mysteriously acquired funds for the Church. New dies for gold coins had arrived from England. Gold pieces in denominations of $5, $10, and $20 were appearing in large numbers. Construction on the Mormon temple, once slowed because of the high cost of freight to bring in building material, suddenly speeded up.

In the tightly knit society, an

CALEB RHODES

enigmatic joint-petition by Rhoades and Brigham Young from the Territorial Legislature for a large tract of mountainous land at the confluence of Weber River and Beaver Creek below Hoyt Peak aroused curiosity. It has been said that curiosity abruptly abated when one who followed Rhoades on a mysterious trek didn't live to nourish regrets!

Following Thomas Rhoades's death in 1869, the secret of the mine passed to his son Caleb. The younger Rhoades was by nature more enterprising than his father. Aware of one Spanish mine, he suspected more. Before long, he managed to coerce an Indian friend into revealing others abandoned by the Spanish who had enslaved early Utes.

Those mines, unfortunately for Caleb, were located on land then reserved for Indians. To free them from reservation status required an act of Congress. The enormity of the wealth of Brigham's mine is evidenced by an offer Caleb presented to Congress in 1897. In exchange for the release of claims he wished to develop on the reservation, Caleb agreed to pay the United States' national debt with gold from Brigham's mine. The national debt then amounted to $250,000,000! An agreement was duly signed in Washington, but years of governmental red tape delayed the formal opening of the deleted reservation lands until September 1905—three months too late to take advantage of Rhoades's agreement to cancel the national debt. Caleb Rhoades had died on June 2nd. With him died the secret location of the famous Mormon Mine.

Denis's and my determination to cut our way along a barely discernible old trail into Hoyt Canyon was short lived, but it most assuredly invited our respect for those hardy Spanish explorers who opened up this country in the 1700s and for the miners who stayed to sink shafts.

Retreating to the comfort of our Range Rover, we followed a primitive road leading to the summit of Hoyt Peak. Scratches we suffered in the canyon below were forgiven.

Now undergrowth gave way to a clean range splashed with mountain bluebell, lupin and vivid Indian paintbrush. We followed foot paths beside old creek beds and bounced up rutted trails jutting off from the primary four-wheel-drive road. At the summit, where pine-scented air all but crackled with purity, we cooked weinies on the tailgate and gazed long and hard at misty mountains cascading like ancient Japanese prints into more misty mountains. We had a memorable day, but we did not find Brigham's bonanza. Perhaps we had initiated our search in the wrong place—a conclusion which demanded a return trip to Hoyt Peak.

In late September, accompanied by Trent Lowe and his sons Erik and Alex, our Range Rover again grunted up to the peak through Hoyt Canyon. This time our focus was sharper. We now carried a topographical map and an out-of-print used book that described early Spanish mining methods. We consulted a list of clues as we drove along.

First were directional signals carved into aspen trees. Early Spanish miners employed a universal code to identify trails, just as we use highway markers today. A heftless arrow on an upward slant meant to follow in that direction until the next sign. If the arrow was

A standardized series of directional signals was traditionally employed by illiterate early Spanish prospectors and carved into canyon walls or trees. The slightly inclined arrow without a heft, as seen above, indicated that other directional signs lay further on. The two vertical lines might have shown distance, such as two varas. Remember that these early miners were on horseback, so look higher than your head for signs. The one pictured is well above the reach of an average man.

accompanied by vertical or horizontal lines, they denoted the number of *varas* (approximately three miles) until the next sign. A heftless arrow carved in a horizontal position indicated that a mine lay camouflaged in the vicinity. A serpentine sign going up a tree meant to travel on to the next sign from the opposite side of the tree.

Anyone fighting his way through the lethal maze of undergrowth in Hoyt Canyon would have had to blaze a trail to ever return. Even at higher elevations where the undergrowth is less dense, we found it impossible to relocate a sign we had noted only a few months earlier. When Thomas and Caleb Rhoades later created different approaches to the mine, they no doubt blazed distinctive signs of their own. Possibly the repetition of a sign different from the Spaniards' would indicate theirs.

Distinguishing old signs from modern graffiti is difficult. We warned the boys to consider only those carved into mature, large aspen trunks and to keep in mind that

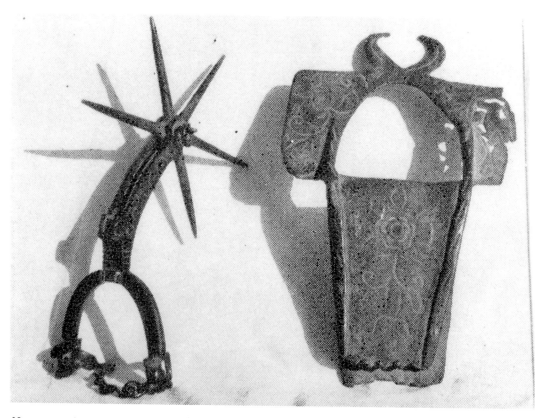

Numerous Spanish relics have been found in the Uintas. In addition to those above, hikers have recovered iron tools, buckskin packsacks, cast-iron melting pots and retorts, a crossbow and pieces of armor.

50

signs carved by Spanish miners astride a mule would appear considerably higher than modern ones. Aspen growth occurs from the top of the tree, so a sign carved a century or more ago would remain at its original height, but the circumference of the trunk would be considerably enlarged.

We were interpreting a series of high vertical carvings as Spanish vara signs when Erik, our Boy Scout, set us straight. They were bear-claw scratches, a solution soon substantiated when we met a bear and her cub on the Hoyt Canyon road.

Old trails also are important clues, sometimes only indicated by a line of trees lower than surrounding ones. Road makers have always followed the path of least resistance. When Mormons first cut wagon trails into Uinta's pastureland, you can be sure that they followed trails first traveled by Spanish pack trains.

A third clue we considered was presented by Utah historian-writer George A.

Not too many years ago, and still today, some historians claim that the presence of early Spaniards as far north as Utah's Uintas is poppycock. Don't you believe it.

In 1776, Franciscan padres Escalante and Dominquez set forth to discover a route that would connect Spanish settlements in New Mexico with Monterey, California. They failed to reach their final destination, but their efforts launched the old Spanish Trail from which variations opened new territory for exploration and travel by others. Those famed Franciscan priests were not first to enter Utah, however.

Two hundred years earlier, in 1540 under the command of Coronado, a Spanish conquistador named Lopez de Cardenas had reached the Colorado River northeast of where the river crosses into Arizona from southern Utah. Records found in the Archives de la Nacion at Mexico City and in the Archives of the Indies at Seville, Spain, suggest that he was followed by another expedition in 1621, accompanied by a Father Geronimo Salmeron, whose journal identified Mt. Timpanogos, Utah Lake and the Wasatch Range where he found rich mines of silver, copper, lead and lodestone already illicitly worked by his countrymen. Numerous small parties of miners carried on covert explorations into uncharted lands that went officially unrecorded to avoid paying the Royal Fifth.

Thompson. His findings concluded that Thomas Rhoades used to make his trek from Salt Lake City to the mine and back in two weeks, leading sixteen pack animals. This indicates that Rhoades's time was spent in loading, rather than mining, which in turn suggests that the ore was already refined and reserved inside the mine to await transport to Mexico by mule train. Thus a proximity of the mine to water and pastureland would have been a requisite while Spaniards engaged in the process of refining ore.

Did Brigham's bonanza lie near here? A suspicious mound rises beside the road just beyond the confluence of the two routes up to Hoyt Peak. Where the dirt came from to form the mound is a mystery, since no cavity exists in the immediate area.

Two trails ascend up to Hoyt Peak from the Kamas area. Old journals tell of the Rhoades's occasionally stopping on treks to the mine to visit with farmers along both routes. A trail from Kamas passes through Hoyt Canyon; the other runs north from neighboring Samak (Kamas spelled backwards). The trails meet at a point about midway up the peak. Our last clue suggests that Brigham's Mormon Mine lies above, if not near, the confluence of the two trails. In his latter years, Caleb Rhoades moved to Vernal, Utah. It was noted that when he visited his mine following that move, he entered the Hoyt Peak area from Samak. Earlier he had entered it from Hoyt Canyon. This may have depended upon trail conditions, but since they ultimately converge, it appears that his targeted area lay beyond the confluence. One route up is as convenient as the other and both fall within the land grant framed by the confluence of Weber River and Beaver Creek petitioned by Rhoades and Brigham Young in 1858.

At a spot just slightly above the confluence of the two trails, we noted a large, man-made mound rising above the ground's surface. Denis stopped the car and we all piled out to investigate. Could it be tailings? Close inspection proved it so old that rock and soil had amalgamated into a covering too hard to dig with our equipment.

Now when those early Spaniards dug their shafts, the debris they dug up had to go someplace. Canny as they were at disguising their mines, could they have packed the tale-tell loads on their mules to cart away? No cavity within proximity of the mound revealed a source from which the dirt to form it had come.

The top of Hoyt Peak in the Uintas

Spanish mines of that era were typically constructed with two tunnels that connected underground to one vertical shaft from which small rooms, protected by heavy timber doors, served as work and storage rooms for gold bars awaiting mule train transportation to Sonora. According to old documents, an average of forty Spanish miners oversaw the slaves and engaged in processing ore. This indicates a sizable camp. The suspicious mound we now examined rose amid a wide clearing that could have accommodated both men and cattle.

Bordering it on the west, an ancient streambed formed a dry trough. To its east, on the edge of the clearing, a shallower streambed once carried water from an unknown source. While the boys checked the area with a metal detector, I followed an old trail which soon faded into a mass of forested undergrowth. Could it have led to a concealed mine shaft?

Spanish miners were masterful when it came to camouflage, as witnessed by the skill with which Peralta concealed the Arizona mine known as the Lost Dutchman. Once Caleb Rhoades had removed the ready supply of gold here, he could have resealed the old Mormon Mine even more effectively, employing cement and milling tools unavailable to the earlier miners.

When Denis and I initially probed the secret of Hoyt Peak, melting snow rendered the soppy clay ground too slippery for climbing. Now in autumn's sunshine, chill winds rendered it too cold for the apparel we wore. This brought to an end our hunt for gold at Hoyt Peak, as it no doubt did for those early Spaniards who worked the Uintas in the summer, but moved to their mines in southern Utah and Arizona during the wrathful winters. For Hoyt Peak, at an altitude of 10,226 feet, is blanketed by snow ten feet deep at least six months of the year. To warrant working a mine in a climate known to have dropped to -20°F, it would have to reap rich rewards. Utahan Buck Williams, whose family has had a cabin in the area for over a hundred years, emphasizes the callous winters with a true story about an old trapper who lived there in the 1860s.

How and where the old man found a bride was a mystery, but when he did, he brought her to live in his lonely cabin beside a stream. Barely had the blush left her cheeks when the bride succumbed to a fatal illness. Although the laconic old man was accustomed to living without conversation, he missed her physical presence. So what he did was put her out to freeze while he set his beaver traps, then brought her in for company at dinner. Thus life went on as usual until summer thaws rendered the ground soft enough to dig a grave.

In view of winters like that, anyone seeking the lost Mormon Mine is well advised to confine his search to summer months.

As the trail reaches higher toward Hoyt Peak, the underbrush thins out and there would have been room for the Spanish miners to pasture their pack mules.

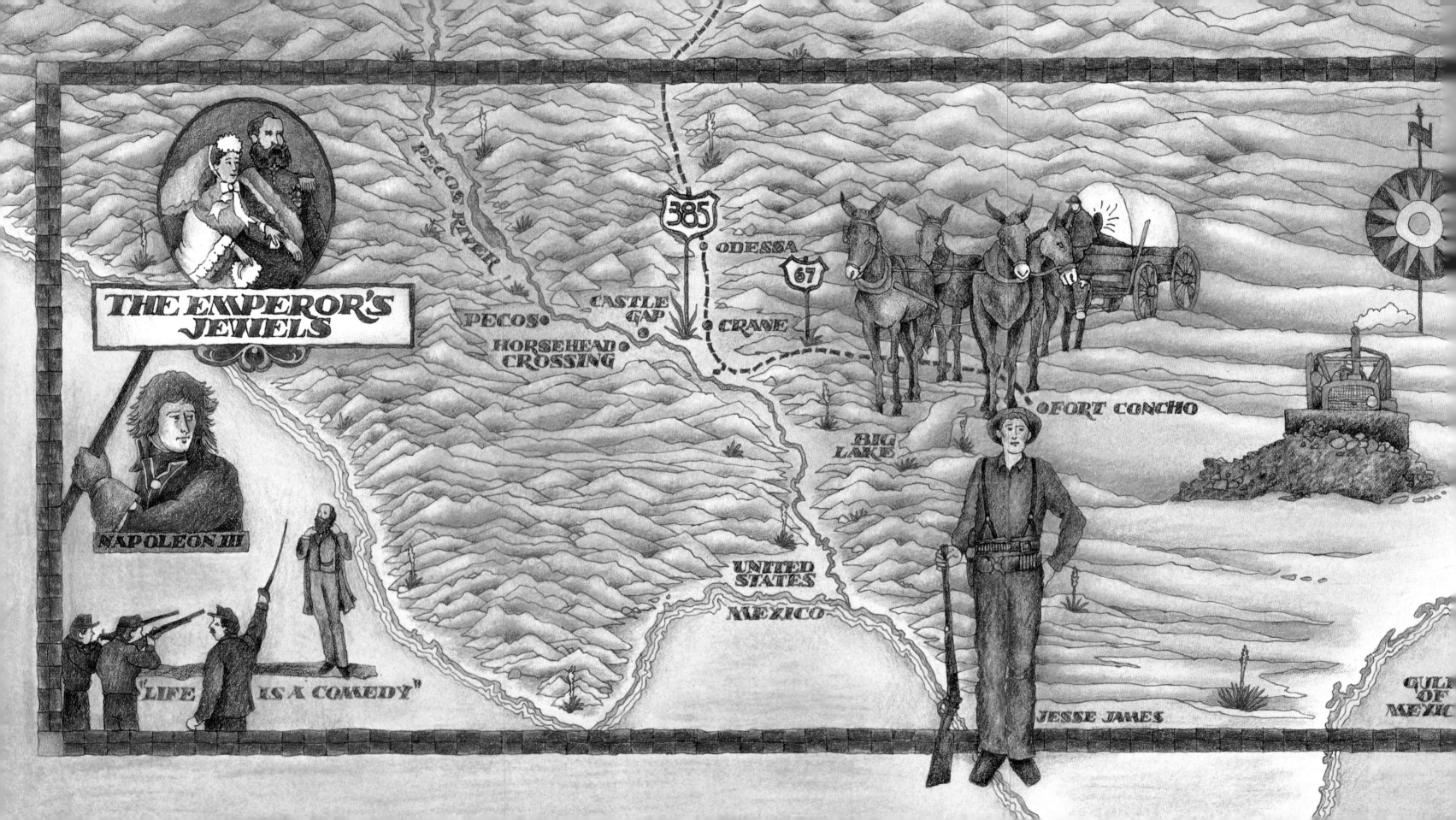

THE EMPEROR'S JEWELS

Somewhere in the eroded, dusty ranch country between Castle Gap and old Fort Concho in Texas lies buried a cache of jewels worthy of an emperor. Near them, bleached by over a century of hot sun, may also lie burned relics of an old wagon caravan and scattered human bones—testimony to the sneakiest, if not richest, jewel heist in the West.

To account for the precious cargo being there in the first place, we have to go back to 1864, when Napoleon III used his influence to boost Maximilian, an Austrian

Carlota and Maximilian landing in Mexico to begin their short reign as emperor and empress.

Archduke of the Hapsburg family, to the Imperial throne of the newly established Empire of Mexico. By actively supporting the new emperor and his Empress Carlota, Napoleon hoped that France would regain the prestige it had lost in North America over the Louisiana Purchase.

Bringing their entire Austrian fortunes with them, the new rulers spared no expense in creating an Imperial court worthy of the mightiest sovereign. Maximilian lavishly restored the old Spanish Chapultepec Castle in Mexico City; his power-hungry Carlota ran the affairs of the state. For three years they were a happy couple. Then Napoleon III had a change of heart.

Napoleon had hoped that an Imperial court would create order in Mexico's traditionally chaotic political arena, but after his army had supported Maximilian for three years, Mexico was still asunder. Fanatic guerrillas, led by the liberal Benito Juarez, overran the country. Napoleon knew that without French army protection, the new empire would crumble, but the army was now needed in Europe, so he recalled it from Mexico.

Desperate, Carlota embarked for France to plead for more time. Napoleon scorned her appeal. The puissant woman could not handle defeat. Hopeless and powerless, she lost her mind. When the tragic news reached Maximilian in Mexico, he was devastated. "My wife is mad," he cried. "These people are killing me by inches. I am

Carlota, the Belgian princess who became Empress of Mexico.

thoroughly worn out. I am going home."

His departure was interrupted by a let-
ter from his mother in Austria. The former
Austrian archduke's position in Europe
would be ridiculous if he abdicated, the
powerful archduchess counseled. What of
Hapsburg honor? And what would be the
fate of his loyal supporters if he took
flight? Better that he bury himself in
Mexico than come home a failure.

Maximilian vacillated. One decision
appeared as hopeless as the other. At last
he acquiesced to his mother.

Meanwhile, more and more Mexican
towns were surrendering to rampaging
bands of Juarez's guerrilla liberals. Smoke

billowed above the burning homes of empire supporters as their last protection, the
French soldiers, left the country. Abandoned in his castle with only a few remaining
Austrian loyalists, Maximilian courageously faced the future. Within a week of the
French troop's departure, he also left, but not in flight.

Wearing the coat of a Mexican general, a sombrero, dark trousers, kneeboots, two
revolvers and a saber, Maximilian rode at the head of nine thousand men walking in
straggling groups, unprotected by any kind of flank guard. The "Imperial Mexican
Army" he had managed to assemble was marching forth to challenge the empire's liberal enemies upon a field of honor. Half of his men were raw recruits, hastily shep-
herded by fourteen-year-old lieutenants and officers of higher rank, resplendent in gold
lace and stiff tunic collars. For arms, they carried pikes, hatchets, swords, old Enfields,
battered muskets, discarded French pieces and Austrian pistols.

Only one European soldier rode with Maximilian, an Austrian aristocrat. All other
European soldiers loyal to the emperor were ordered to remain with his treasures in
Mexico City. Maximilian wanted no stigma of "foreign support" or "imperialistic trap-
pings" to demean this battle to unite his chosen country.

As if predestined for martyrdom, his naivety in warfare manifested itself on the first
battleground at Queretaro. The Imperial army found itself trapped as in the bottom of
a teacup, surrounded on all sides by enemy-occupied mountains.

If Maximilian's weakness was vanity, he had no lack of courage. At night he wrapped himself in a serape and slept beside his men on the rocky, cactus-covered ground. He suffered violently with dysentery. He ate mule and cat meat. A safe escape was arranged, but he refused to leave for as long as one soldier stood. The Imperial army held out for seventy-one days.

When at last Maximilian surrendered to the guerrilla leaders, his friends in Mexico City sent three prominent lawyers to plead for his life. Regardless, he was condemned to death. As he passed before the seven-man firing squad, he presented to each of its members a gold coin carrying his profile. "Here is where I wanted to plant the standard of victory, and it is here where I am going to die. Life is only a comedy," he wryly observed.

Word of the execution had not yet reached Mexico City. Gambling that the attorneys they had sent would succeed in sparing Maximilian's life so he could be exiled to Austria, a party of Imperial supporters was already bound for the Texas border with Maximilian's treasures. Gold bullion, Spanish, Austrian, and American coins, vessels of gold and silver and jewels approximating five million dollars had been concealed in forty-five flour barrels. The caravan, consisting of four Austrian noblemen and fifteen peons, hoped to reach the safe harbor at Galveston, Texas, from where the treasure could be shipped to Maximilian's castle in Europe.

The caravan had miraculously eluded Mexican patriots through the long, northward trek in rural Mexico when they encountered a band of six ex-Confederate soldiers traveling south into Mexico on the same Chihuahua Trail. The one Austrian who spoke English consulted them about road conditions on the Texas Trail that lay ahead. Upon learning that Horsehead Crossing and Castle Gap seethed with hostile Indians and bandits, the Austrian asked if the soldiers would be willing to reverse their trek and accompany his caravan as guides and guards to protect a valuable cargo of flour—for adequate compensation, of course.

Indeed, the soldiers would be willing! Their first few nights passed safely. Then, shortly after crossing Pecos River in southwestern Texas at Horsehead Crossing, one of the ex-Confederate guards grew curious. He had noticed that during daylight hours the wagon drivers never left their seats and at night one always slept on each of the tightly covered wagons. Strange, he whispered to his comrades, that plain old barrels of flour should demand such protection. His comrades agreed.

That night, while Maximilian's men slept, the soldiers diverted the attention of an Austrian guard to alleviate their curiosity. Once a barrel was pried open and its contents revealed, the fate of Maximilian's party was sealed.

For ragged soldiers to risk transporting such a vast hoard of riches would be folly. Their only chance to escape the attention of bandits along the trail would be to secure the barrel's contents in a place to which they could safely return without a protective force. Castle Gap's mile-long pass amid rocky spires and cavities was not such a place.

Maximilian, the Austrian archduke who became Emperor of Mexico.

This gateway, infamous for harboring legions of outlaws, still echoed with Comanche war whoops. Only recently an entire herd of the Texas Goodnight-and-Loving cattle ranch had been eradicated while trying to pass through. Best they keep the Austrian party intact until after Castle Gap was behind them, the soldiers decided.

Unaware of impending treachery, the Austrians relaxed in the care of their Confederate guides, and the burdened caravan struggled through tortuous Castle Gap. But a night or two later, at a campsite near a body of water not far off the trail, the Austrian party was eliminated, its wagons fired, the bodies burned. Only the contents of the barrels, buried for future recovery, were spared.

After stuffing saddlebags with enough coins to meet their immediate needs, the tired soldiers took careful note of rocks, sand, a lake and other distinctive landmarks. They then dragged themselves across the sere desert toward Concho River. Never again would Maximilian's treasures grace a castle in Austria!

Upon arrival at Fort Concho (now San Angelo), a chronic ailment forced one of the soldiers to tarry until he became strong enough to rejoin his comrades at a rendezvous in San Antonio. However, fearing that he might lose out while they conjured up a plan to covertly dispense of the jewels, he set forth alone before recovering fully. To his shock, a mere day's ride beyond Fort Concho, he came upon their mutilated bodies strewn along the road. Whether Indians or bandits were responsible, he did not pause to determine. All he knew now was that he was the sole owner of Maximilian's treasure and that advantageously disposing of it without arousing suspicion would require professional help.

When the French artillery sent to Mexico by Napoleon III was withdrawn and the new empire left without European support, Carlota went mad and Maximilian failed.

As he rode slowly along the trail pondering that problem, the name of an ex-Civil War buddy and fellow Missourian came to mind. Jesse James, the notorious outlaw, had not yet reached the apex of his ignoble career, but still had a reputation suggestive of unsavory ventures. To contact James, however, would necessitate a change of venue. So, instead of continuing along the trail to San Antonio, the only surviving member who was party to the burying of Maximilian's jewel cache turned his horse toward St. Louis, his hometown.

He had ridden as far as Denton, Texas, when the chronic malady that plagued him reasserted itself. This time it was fatal. The ex-soldier's final days were witnessed by a Dr. Black, who treated him, and a lawyer named Conner. Just before dying, he gasped out the story of the buried millions near Castle Gap.

According to famous Texas chronicler Frank Dobie, Dr. Black was given a map, but when he and the lawyer launched a treasure hunt after they had retired many years later, violent sandstorms common to the area had shifted the landscape. A lake noted on the map did not exist. Nor did other landmarks match the terrain around Castle Gap, where Dr. Black was led to believe the massacre had occurred.

The nearest lake to Castle Gap lies beside a town known today as Big Lake, some forty miles east of Castle Gap, but en route to where the ailing man had parted from his friends at Fort Concho. For the past twenty years the lake has been dry. Since it and Castle Gap are the only distinctive landmarks in the otherwise featureless, flat scape that the Austrians and their ex-Confederate guards passed through between Horsehead Crossing and Fort Concho, it would not be surprising that the sequence of events became blurred in the sick man's mind. The massacre of the Austrians could have occurred as the party approached Big Lake, rather than at Horsehead Crossing or the Gap itself, where Dr. Black understood it had happened.

Both of the latter sites have been thoroughly explored by treasure seekers. Horsehead Crossing on the Pecos River, once a treacherous waterway cursed with quicksand, is today choked with salt cedar and depleted of water due to irrigation. In spite of a century of fruitless treasure hunts, its ranch lands still get pocked with holes.

As for Castle Gap, in 1968 two determined Texans bulldozed a gully forty feet deep, eight feet wide and one-hundred-eight feet long through it—abundant testimony to the scores of treasure seekers who, like Dr. Black, pursued Maximilian's jewels in the wrong place.

Approximately forty-five miles east of Castle Gap on Highway 67, en route to Fort Concho, lies the illusive bed of Big Lake. It is not surprising that Dr. Black and his companion failed to see it. Even today's travelers on Highway 67—which crosses Reagan County within two miles of the three-mile-long, one-mile-wide lake that once covered two thousand acres—often fail to see it. Old-timers claim that the lake, which had no outlet, always contained water until oil wells were drilled in the Big Lake Oil Field in the 1920s. Folklore, however, suggests that the lake only fills every twenty years, and then mysteriously empties. The last substantial stand of water appeared in 1974, but disappeared three years later.

Considering the lake's "here today, gone tomorrow" history, it is little wonder that Dr. Black and those who followed considered the soldier's map misleading, and ignored his portrayal of a non-existent body of water.

If I were to devote a few days to jewel hunting in western Texas, I would look around for a suspicious rock or earth formation, possibly manmade, in an area west of Big Lake. The barrels, emptied of treasure and set afire, would render the real treasure site as no more promising than an old campfire.

Nothing is certain, but some factors remain clear. Maximilian's men did escort his fabulous treasures beyond the Pecos at Horsehead Crossing; they were killed prior to reaching Fort Concho; and Mexico's former Crown Jewels lie buried in Texas sand.

Maximilian (on right) as he cited his last words before the firing squad, "Life is a comedy!"

THE 200-POUND CACHE

here's a two-hundred-pound stash of gold buried up here and I know a guy who knows where it is." Frank Maggio's voice crackled with excitement. He was calling long distance from Elko, Nevada, where he was on a magazine assignment to photograph a rodeo.

During the three years I lived in Las Vegas, Maggio and I occasionally worked as a writer-photographer team, but I wasn't about to drive up to Elko from Las Vegas on a

wild goose chase. "Why doesn't he find it himself?"

"It's a great story," Frank went on. "We'll make all the arrangements . . . you just get up here tomorrow."

"Who's 'we'?"

"A rodeo wrangler, a guy named Tom. He knows the country like the back of his hand . . ."

Maggio and I had met at a guest ranch in 1960 when we both were new arrivals to Las Vegas. In a burst of enthusiasm one day I bought a horse and talked the *Las Vegas Sun* into letting me

do a series of "discovering the desert by horseback" stories for the newspaper's Sunday magazine section. Maggio, who had been an official White House staff photographer before coming west, volunteered to illustrate the features with photos. In those days Las Vegas bankers still wore ten-gallon hats, and ranch motifs were more commonplace than pyramids and volcanoes, so Maggio's promise of a "good story" with a western angle proved irresistible. I threw my favorite saddle into the station wagon and took off for Elko.

When I arrived at the old Star Hotel there, my "podner's" Stetson was hanging over the bar alongside a rangy cowboy who looked like a model for a Marlboro cigarette ad. The plan, they informed me, was to head out at dawn for a ranch in Independence Valley that was lending us horses. Elko County is one of the few places where cattlemen and miners meet on the same playing field, so it wasn't illogical that a cache of gold should be buried in this vast ranch country, which also includes the Tuscarora mining district. "It's somewhere along McCann Creek," cowboy Tom confidently informed us.

That was his last show of confidence throughout a nine-hour horseback ride. For, rather than an old Nevada cowhand, cowboy Tom proved to be an itinerant, albeit picturesque, rodeo fixture whose only knowledge of the buried cache was what he heard at the corral. Not only was he vague about the legend, he couldn't tell McCann Creek from Pleasant Creek, Boulder Creek, Adams Creek or any of the countless other creeks that cut across this valley.

Miners of the Tuscarora district were a hearty bunch in 1880.

The upshot of the experience was that Maggio got a free ride back to Las Vegas and I learned three important things about treasure hunting: always have a detailed map of the area; research the story first; and never trust a guy "who knows the country like the back of his hand."

Thirty-three years later, I embarked upon another search for this same elusive treasure—this time in a Range Rover accompanied by my husband Denis and my uncle Bob Carleson and his wife Jean. Bob, a retired Salt Lake City Cadillac dealer, once had an agency in Elko. When Denis and I asked if he'd like to join us, Bob said the magic words. "You bet! I know that country *like the back of my hand!*"

Not one to get caught in the same web twice, I obtained a U.S. Geological Survey map of Tuscarora and boned up on the legend of the Idahoan's buried two-hundred-pound cache of gold.

The legend's trail leads back in time to 1864 when seven men set out from Silver City, Idaho, on a well-equipped prospecting expedition into Nevada. Having no luck along the Owyhee River as they followed it south into Nevada, they proceeded into the west side of Independence Valley where, upon reaching McCann Creek, they lucked out.

The placer site they found there proved so rich that they split into teams, one half of the party mining while the others constructed a camp and corral. This was dangerous Shoshone country, so they also erected a precautionary stone breastwork in the event of Indian attack. By the time their camp was made comfortable, the men already had accumulated some two hundred pounds of gold.

Hardly had they laid a last stone on the defensive wall when one of the party detected an Indian scout spying upon them from a distant hill. That night the seven men debated around the fire. Their supply of ammunition was ample and their camp

well located for defense. Should they chance defending themselves? Or should they risk two of their members by sending to Idaho for help?

Indians often dispersed fast when the bullets started to fly. The men figured that five of them could hold out long enough to force a temporary retreat if the attack occurred

All social life was not confined to Tuscarora's bawdy houses and hell-raising saloons. The town also boasted of a social center named Plunkett's Hall that employed a novel tilting floor used flat for dances, but tipped down at one end to effect a stage for theatrical affairs. The Virginia City Opera House with its floor supported by railroad car springs, a ballet dancing school, an elocution teacher, two skating rinks and a school with classes from grade one to ten contributed other spurts of culture and entertainment to the isolated settlement that produced over $30 million in gold and silver before its decline in 1907.

before help arrived, but whether or not Lady Luck would carry two riders through Shoshone country safely with $100,000 worth of gold was a major risk. Another concern was that they might expose their strike before they had exhausted it for themselves. If the riders did succeed in getting through with the gold, it would create a minor gold rush from Idaho to their Nevada camp.

As the last ember of fire burned out, they reached a decision. The gold cache had a better chance of survival if left with the five men. Thus the two best riders of the party saddled their horses and stealthily headed north in the dark of night.

Heedless of danger, they cut as direct a trail through the rough country as possible. The old Owyhee Toll Road from Silver City was not completed until two years later, so the men were picking a trail through relatively uncharted terrain. That they avoided capture by the Shoshones before arriving at their destination was somewhat miraculous.

Silver City, Idaho, was in its initial throes of optimism. Two years after this incident it would become the Owyhee County seat, but in 1864 the rich War Eagle Mine and the illustrious Poorman vein had just been discovered. The seven Nevada-bound prospectors had been popular figures in Idaho mining communities. When the two riders called for help, a sizable party responded.

Unfortunately, it was too late. The rescue party arrived at the Nevada camp on McCann Creek to find nothing left but the ravaged bodies of five men. According to a report in the *Elko Independent*, the brave prospectors, protected by their breastworks, had "kept the Indians at bay for several days, killing many of them as they charged upon the little fortification." But with all five men dead, there was no one left to report how much warning of attack the men had had or of what measures they took to protect their cache of gold. The two returning members of the original team searched in vain.

Three years later, in 1867, a rich gold deposit was discovered in the same general

Today, not even a ghost is left in Tuscarora.

area and the town of Tuscarora was born. Among those who followed the new strike were the two riders of the earlier party. Unlike most of the arriving prospectors, this pair was more interested in recovering a fortune already mined than in digging up a new one.

Finding the Shoshones now in a more docile mood, they located a member of the

earlier raiding party and coerced him into describing the attack. He assured them that no gold had been found on or near the site of the killings. Because the two survivors had thoroughly examined what was left of the camp upon their arrival after the massacre, they had to assume that their friends had buried the gold somewhere nearby prior to the attack.

The *Elko Independent* in 1870 reported that the gold strike originally worked by the seven men from Idaho had been relocated and was of "wonderful richness in both gold and silver." But still, the cache of gold that those men died trying to protect has remained unfound for over a century.

Now our little modern-day prospecting party hoped to change that.

Brief bursts of sunshine interrupted the cloudy sky as we sloshed up the muddy road to Tuscarora. Torrents of rain had preceded us; more would undoubtedly follow. But inclement weather has never yet cured a case of gold fever. Bob Carleson had his father's (my grandfather's) old pan for winnowing gold at the ready; metal detectors in the car's trunk presaged treasure for our initiate prospector, Denis.

The Tuscarora cemetery which we passed turned out to be as lively as anything in town. Heavy equipment rested nearby and a few occupied residences suggested that mines are still operative in the district, but apparently not on rainy days.

Little else remains to reflect the wild old town's early shoot-'em-up reputation. Founded in 1867 by two brothers, John and Steven Beard, the fanciful name of Tuscarora was bestowed upon the town by an old-time prospector who once had served as a sailor on a U.S. gunboat of that name. All present liked its sound, so the name stuck. A ditch was dug through McCann Canyon to carry water to the diggings and by 1871 the Tuscarora mining district was hailed throughout the West for its surface placer gold.

The dilemma our party now faced was in locating the probable campsite of those Idahoan prospectors who hid their cache of gold. Considering that they came upon McCann Creek from Independence Valley, was their campsite southeast of Tuscarora, or southwest? McCann Creek cuts a long channel as Bob, who knew the country *"like the back of his hand,"* was learning. On my earlier fiasco with cowboy Tom and Maggio we had covered the southeast area. Denis now prudently followed an old mining road southwest of the early town site that followed McCann Creek towards a rise designated on our topo map as Battle Mountain. It, I had read, was named for the Indian skirmish with the Idahoans.

Discovering where the Idahoans established their camp would not determine the site of their hidden cache, but it would provide us with a starting point for the search. Two foregone conclusions worked in our favor. The men had to have been within a convenient distance to water, necessary to their placer operation; and their camp had to be within sight of Battle Mountain if, indeed, that was where the skirmish with the Indians had occurred.

It struck us that the most obvious clue would be to find some semblance of the protective breastwork the men had built. Had it been constructed of wood, it would have gone the way of a century of campfires. But it was not. It was built of rock, of no use to man or beast. Mountains in this area are little more than rounded hills with few protective barriers, as compared to rugged, jagged ranges elsewhere in the West. Any defensive measures had to be of the Idahoan's own fabrication, with only two strategic courses appearing plausible. Either they erected their defense high on a barren hill so they could pop off the enemy as it ascended; or, they avoided exposure down by the creek amid a clump of trees, as old Jim Bowie once held off an Indian attack down in Texas.

While we debated where to start looking, a rumble in the heavens influenced a quick decision. Denis

Other placer miners came later, but these six could well have been the Idahoans.

and Bob aimed their metal detectors towards a sheltered, verdant spot where McCann Creek takes a turn north in the direction of Battle Mountain. To Bob's delight, he received an immediate reading. Jean retrieved a shovel from the car and Denis started to dig, and dig, and dig. Meanwhile, rain fell, and fell, and fell. Then, joy of joys, the shovel hit something solid. The metal detector buzzed madly. Bob yelled, "One thing for sure, it's more than a tin can!"

You bet it was. It was a large chunk of iron ore. Not exactly the treasure we were seeking, but a good paperweight. Bob wanted to hike up Battle Mountain to see if his detector would uncover remains of rifle shells left from the battle, but worsening weather hampered any further exploration.

As for the two-hundred-pound cache, it doesn't necessarily lie buried at the Idahoan's campsite—nor even on the same side of the creek. As pointed out earlier, terrain here is not given to caves or likely cavities for secreting plunder. Would the

Battle Mountain, reportedly named for the Indian skirmish with the Idahoans.

Idahoans have crossed the creek to camouflage their cache in a sage-covered hole; or kept it close to camp; or carried it up one of the low mountains that frame the creek? Five men with sturdy horses could have transported the gold a safe distance from camp, but the mere contemplation of sites creates a mental maze tangled enough to defy Ariadne's golden thread.

This cache will be found accidentally, I wager, probably by a hiker after the ground has been stirred by winter snows. If anything remains of the breastwork, old campfires, indications of a corral or spent ammunition from the Indian conflict, we failed to find it. Nevertheless, the magnificent country, hued with silvery-green sage, gold-tinted earth and the music of McCann Creek rippling over rocky rills, more than compensated us for forfeiting the weighty treasure to a future finder.

We came home wet, muddy and empty handed, but far from discouraged. Treasure hunting is like that. Next time. . . .

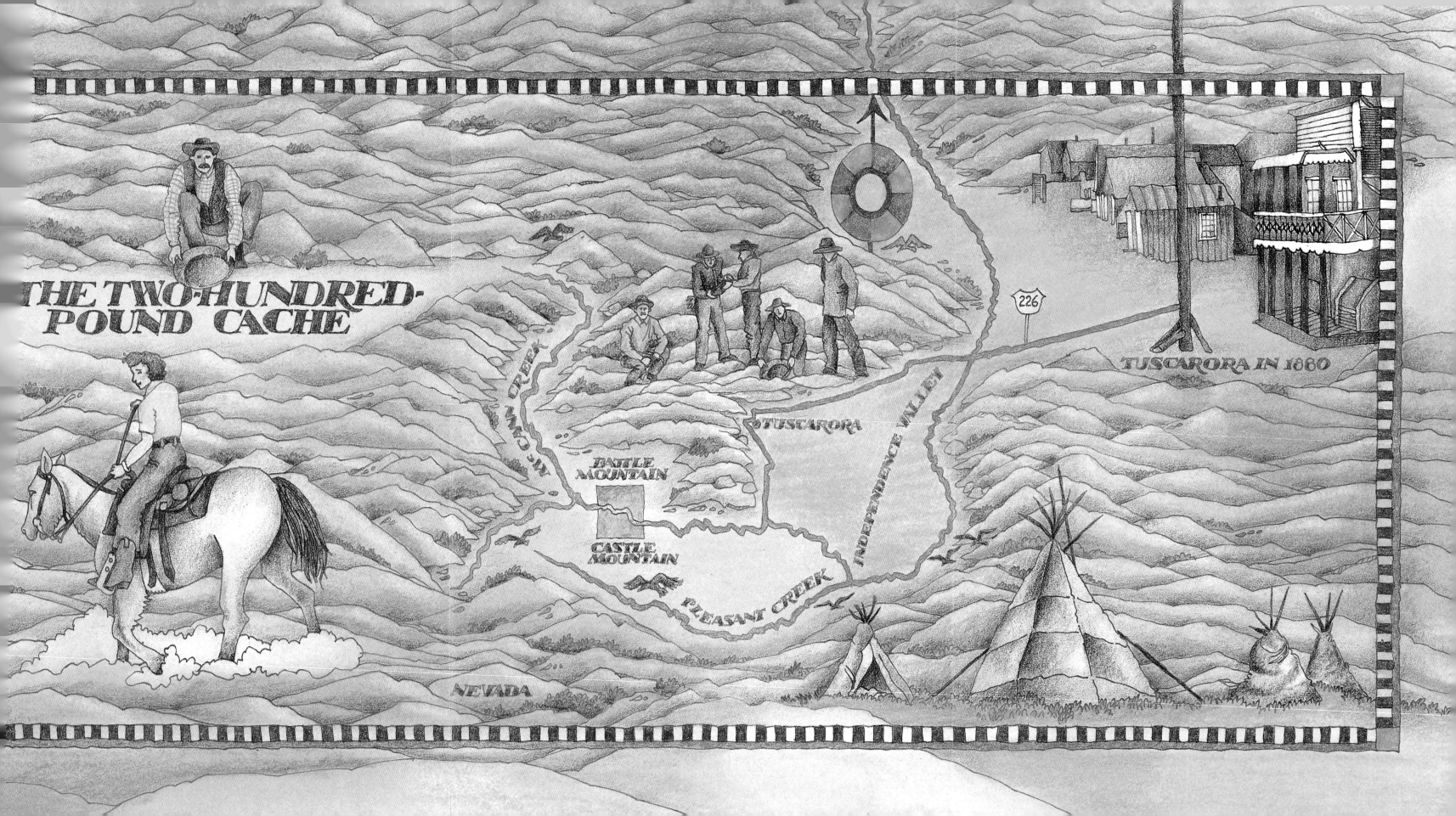

THE TWO·HUNDRED·
POUND CACHE

NEVADA

MC CANN CREEK

BATTLE
MOUNTAIN

CASTLE
MOUNTAIN

TUSCARORA

PLEASANT CREEK

INDEPENDENCE VALLEY

226

TUSCARORA IN 1880

NOISY MOUNTAIN'S SILENT SECRET

hy David Jamison, an unemployed Scotsman totally inexperienced in rugged terrain, would choose Cerro Ruido in which to seek lost Spanish treasure when he drifted into Arizona in the fall of 1922, makes about as much sense as blindly dropping a pea on a map to choose a destination. He knew nothing about the area except that it lay just above the Mexican border and was not far from the home of an American friend, Bill Walters, who lived in Tucson.

Upon arriving in Tucson, Jamison imposed upon his friend to drive him to the foothills of the range. Walters tried to persuade him to choose another area. Cerro

Noisy Mountain from the spot where we think Jamison might have established his camp.

Ruido, which means "Noisy Mountain," was shunned by superstitious Indians because of a freak geological structure which emits whistles, like air escaping from a ballast. Walters feared that a wandering Indian hunter might associate Jamison's presence with the mysterious noises and kill him, but Jamison refused to heed such nonsense.

Not only did that danger pose a threat, but Cerro Ruido lies in the Atascosa Mountain Range, just south of the Tumacacori Mountains, and is amid one of the roughest, most cut-up regions in North America. When the U.S. border survey went in to erect a monument there, the men reported that they met with more difficulties than in that same distance along any other part of the Arizona-Mexico boundary. The more Walters tried to discourage Jamison, the more convinced the Scotsman became that it was just the sort of place to find Spanish treasure.

Walters reluctantly deposited Jamison at a spot near the foot of the adjoining Parajitos Mountain, which gave entry to Cerro Ruido. He was relieved to learn that although unemployed, Jamison apparently had some money and the camp he had established was well equipped. Before departing for Tucson, Walters promised to return every few days to check on him and bring fresh supplies.

On the second of those supply runs, Walters was cheered to find Jamison absolutely

The mysterious mission in Cerro Ruido.
—*COURTESY* ARIZONA HIGHWAYS

jubilant. The previous afternoon Jamison reported that he had hiked some ten miles into the mountains and found what appeared to be an ancient trail. Not wanting to get caught in the dark, he had returned to camp, but felt sure the trail would eventually lead to a lost mine. Jamison's excitement was contagious. Walters began to believe maybe Jamison was on to something. Each supply run thereafter became an event to be celebrated as Walters kept pace with Jamison's progress.

Soon after detecting the albeit invisible trail, Jamison had managed to retrace it to the base of a cliff at the foot of Cerro Ruido. The trail led to a mesa midway up the mountain, then completely faded away. Hoping it had just dipped downward and would reappear, Jamison skirted the edge of the mesa. It was then that he saw below him a small canyon where, pinched in the end of a narrow breech, stood a building that appeared to be a mission.

On top of the building were four belfry portals without bells. The building was faced with white stone, similar to the canyon's smooth walls. A solitary palm tree jutted into the sky to the right and rear of the building. Chaparral and mesquite covered the area.

As if it were a mirage, Jamison studied the building for a long time. It did not go away. It was real. He searched the area for a path down to it as long as he dared, but this was an evening when Walters was due to arrive with supplies. Reluctantly, Jamison gave up the search and returned to camp, carefully noting landmarks for his return.

He had read a lot about Spanish conquest in the New World and was aware that in the early days when Spaniards were working mines in Sonora, Mexico, and what is now Arizona, a royal decree demanded that a Franciscan or Jesuit priest must accompany parties licensed to pass beyond the Spanish border of Mexico in order to secure the King's Royal Fifth of any riches recovered. However, numerous small parties of miners carried on covert explorations into unchartered lands that went officially unrecorded for obvious reasons. Tax dodgers they might have been, but less than devout they were not, especially when wily priests were willing to surreptitiously attend to their religious needs.

Since there was no record of an ancient Spanish mission in this particular locale, Jamison guessed that the building he now studied from a distance was more than likely a chapel associated with a mine. Considering the relative majesty of its structure, the mine that supported it must have been very rich indeed!

Getting closer to the site was bound to be a major project. As he slipped and slid downhill through the steep, rocky terrain, he tried to mentally visualize a better way to reach it.

At last, exhausted, he stumbled into camp. Walters waited with a pot of stew bubbling over the fire. Jamison's fatigue disappeared fast as he recounted his incredible experience. The two friends talked far into the night, speculating upon the possibility of a lost church that might harbor old Spanish treasure.

This time, Walters remained overnight. Before departing for Tucson at dawn, he loaded his camera with fresh film and instructed Jamison on how to use it. Jamison then slung a blanket and knapsack over his shoulder and, armed with the camera and a machete, set off early to retrace his trail of the preceding day. Using bearings established then, he was able to reach the opposite side of the canyon by circumventing a rugged formation. Thick mesquite clawed at his clothes and bloody welts rose on his limbs as he hacked his way down a ravine to the canyon floor. By the time he had reached bottom, it was dark. With no desire to fall into some forgotten mine shaft, he laid out his blanket and settled down for the night.

Dawn seemed later than usual because the sun was dulled by gray clouds. Jamison worriedly scanned the sky, knowing that this is one of the most cataclysmic places in the southwest for flash floods. Without taking time for breakfast, Jamison used his machete to cut an approach to the church through the thicket of brambles.

In less than an hour, he came upon a spellbinding sight. The church stood in full view, its four empty belfries ghostly embellishments rising above melted

A side view of the ruins.
—COURTESY ARIZONA HIGHWAYS

adobe walls and an arched doorway. Jamison approached it as if it might evaporate on second sight. He felt himself an intruder into an unwelcome past. Its inviolate facade in the rugged setting reminded him that men much tougher than he had once broken into this land. He poked his machete into a heap of rubble from where parts of the roof had caved in. A rodent scurried from its nest, the only sign of life. Going outside, he traced the contours of the foundation. It extended beyond the front facade where an outbuilding once had adjoined the church, and then turned back to abut the stone walls of the cliff. At that point a jagged crack between two stones in the cliff caught his attention. He almost passed it by, then hesitated. Upon close examination, it became clear that the stones had been mortared into position. He pushed his machete into the crack between them. It was hollow inside.

Jamison chopped frantically at the mortar with his machete. When bits fell away, he hammered upon the obstruction with other stones until the largest of the mortared stones fell inward. Lighting a match, he peered into the cavity. Scores of rotted leather bags lay piled on the floor. With every ounce of strength he possessed, he tried to force the other stone loose so he could at least reach his shoulder into the cave. The effort was futile. It would require more rugged tools than he had at hand.

The storm Walters encountered on his trip back to Tucson.
—*COURTESY* Arizona Highways

Before leaving the site, Jamison removed Walters's camera from his knapsack and photographed the church, the crumbling walls of the outbuilding and the hole he had chopped into the sealed entrance to the cave. Then he slowly hacked his way through the rough chaparral back to camp, mentally noting landmarks that might provide a more direct route for his return.

When Walters arrived late in the afternoon, Jamison intercepted him along the road and broke the good news. They were too excited to wait overnight for Walters to return to Tucson for dynamite, picks and stone chisels. Instead, he unloaded supplies at Jamison's campsite and immediately turned his truck around. As he pulled away, Jamison signaled him to wait while he ran back to the tent to get the camera. He was anxious to see how his photos had come out.

The sky looked ominous even then. Walters figured that they were in for a storm and momentarily wondered if Jamison would be safe out there alone. But no. Jamison had already proven himself capable of coping with the desert. Hopefully the storm would be a short one. Today, signs in the area warn of the floods, but in the twenties no one was expected to be passing that way.

When Walters reached the Don Felipe ranch where the road to Jamison's camp forked onto a main route, a frightening crash of thunder raised the hair on his neck. He stopped the car and looked back. Another violent thunderbolt bounced off Cerro Ruido, offsetting a jagged concourse of lightning. Walters picked up his camera from the seat beside him and used up the remaining film to shoot pictures of the dramatic sky.

At that moment, the heavens let loose with a floodtide that swamped the land around him in one burst. Walters stepped on the starter and raced for Tucson, praying that he could make it before muddy roads tied him up for the night. Later, he admitted that he had only fleetingly worried about the Scotsman. Flash floods are common to the desert. Walters figured that Jamison would know enough to seek high ground and stay there until the storm spun out.

This was the worst storm in the history of the Tucson weather bureau. Nogales on the Arizona-Mexico border reported over a million dollars of damage. Tucson suffered slightly less. Several days passed before Walters dared to attempt the washed-out roads into the Atascosa and Parajito ranges. Meanwhile, he busied himself collecting supplies and equipment for the anticipated expedition into Cerro Ruido where he would remain with Jamison until they had emptied whatever treasure awaited in the cave. Once the skies were peaceful again and most of the floodwater drained from desert roads, Walters left the film from his camera with a local photographer who promised to have the prints ready the following week, and started back to join Jamison in camp. The trip took longer than usual, as he had to scout around for safe detours and remove boulders that now blocked the road.

When he finally arrived at the campsite, it was barely recognizable. The flash flood had swept huge boulders into the level area where Jamison's camp had been, and only a scar remained where they had

constructed a makeshift stone stove. Not even a scattering of debris remained to suggest that the Scotsman had camped there.

Waters sensed what had happened. A tremendous flash flood had erupted from several canyons at once, spewing water as if from a ruptured dam. In his friend's excitement to prepare for their expedition to the treasure cove, he had neglected to prepare for a more immediate danger. While the skies had given warning, both of the mens' minds had been on other things.

Back in Tucson, Walters reported his friend as missing. A search was launched, but Jamison's body was never recovered. About a month later, Walters remembered the film he had left with the photographer. When he examined the photos, they showed clearly what Jamison had found. Using them as a guide, Walters spent years alone looking for the canyon, to no avail. Before he died, he gave the camera and the prints to a younger friend who also searched fruitlessly.

A well-meaning professional treasure hunter recently wrote about the Cerro Ruido lost "mission," claiming that a member of the Arizona Highways staff told him that the photos Jamison purportedly took were phoney. Perhaps I can shed some light on that.

Several generations of staff changes have occurred since the story first appeared in one of the magazine's earliest issues. Many years later, in the 1960s, a television adventure series was made and the producer borrowed the original photos from the magazine to copy for a film set.

I have seen both the original photos and the stills of the movie set. My guess is that they ended up together in the publication's old files and misled a current staff member.

Usually Time lends credence to old treasure legends. In this case, it almost destroyed one.

Jamison figured that the cavity at the bottom of the photo was an entrance into the old mine.
—COURTESY ARIZONA HIGHWAYS

Eventually, in the 1940s, the photographs were reproduced in *Arizona Highways*, a publication issued by the Arizona Department of Highways. Since then, and in recent years, treasure hunters have searched fruitlessly by plane, jeep, horseback and on foot.

In our search, Denis and I located the site of the old ranch that lies at the end of a narrow paved strip on Ruby Road (State 289) just above the Mexican border. From it we followed a rough dirt road to a shady dell looking out upon the Parajitos with Cerro Ruido for a backdrop; very likely the spot in which Jamison established his camp. To scale the steep sides of Cerro Ruido, though, would require climbing skills far superior to ours. So, until someone more determined comes along, Noisy Mountain will retain its silent secret and the church and treasure cavern photographed by Jamison will remain lost.

THE ANATOMY OF A TREASURE LEGEND

A promising lost-treasure quest embodies three essential features—an enticing story, facts that validate the story, and the hope of a worthwhile prize. A treasure hunter equal to uncovering that prize will do a thorough job of exploring these three facets of treasure hunting before plotting a course. To contribute to that end was the aim of this book.

A worthy example of a promising story is that of Charles C. Breyfogle whose adventures in Death Valley gave birth to one of the West's foremost treasure tales. Among the first to tell Breyfogle's story was early mining chronicler J. Ross Browne in the mideighteen hundreds. Scores of others, from Frank Dobie's *Coronado's Children* in the nineteen-thirties to Richard Linginfelter's recent scholarly treatise *Death Valley and the Amargosa*, have elaborated on the story.

Discounting the myriad details of those chroniclers' versions, the crux of the tale

concerns Breyfogle, a powerfully built former New Yorker who wound up broke in Austin, Nevada, in 1862 after investing in a mining camp hotel that, like the mine it accommodated, failed to live up to its promise.

Hoping to replenish his resources, he set forth into California's foreboding Death Valley on the Nevada border. Like numerous prospectors before, Breyfogle was seeking the famous ledge of an earlier traveler who had chipped a rock to repair a gunsight, only to realize that the rock was of pure silver and that he was hopelessly lost in the vast desert.

While gearing up in Austin, Breyfogle learned that a party of three men had recently outfitted for a trek into the same area. He assumed that their mission was the same as his, but when he caught up with them in Death Valley at Mesquite Springs, he found he was wrong. They were Southerners enroute to Texas to enlist in the Confederate Army, and not particularly receptive to his companionship.

Breyfogle tagged along anyway. Death Valley was homeland to hostile Paiutes. Any company was safer than none. Still, at night he kept a discreet distance, bedding down several hundred yards from the Southerners. It was this gesture that saved his life. For at their temporary camp near Stovepipe Wells, he was awakened one night when a hoarse croak, and then a scream, rent the air. Breyfogle determined that a band of Indians was rifling the murdered bodies of his companions. He grabbed his shoes, his miner's pick and fled barefoot down the mountain. Daylight found him on the sere floor of Death Valley, his feet so swollen, torn and sore that he could not put on the carried shoes.

No one knows how many days Breyfogle wandered alone, sick with sunstroke and in an agony of thirst. There were three things a prospector never traveled without—his canteen, his blanket and his burro. Breyfogle had none of these. Somehow he made it to the Funeral Range on the Nevada border of Death Valley. There, three white patches, high on a brooding slope, registered in his foggy mind. White meant limestone. Limestone meant water. As he toiled upward, half delirious, he came to a ledge of quartz. With the rote action of a marathon runner whose mind goes while his legs keep moving, Breyfogle lifted his pick and lopped off a few chunks. He mechanically wrapped the quartz chunks in his bandanna and plodded

A lone prospector braving the ruthless desert between Austin, Nevada, and Death Valley, California.
—PHOTO COURTESY UTAH STATE HISTORICAL SOCIETY

83

J. Ross Browne credited old prospectors with doing more to open up our vast interior territories for settlement and civilization than all the scientific expeditions ever sent across the Rocky Mountains. He called them the "poets" of his century, vagrant spirits whose wealth lay in undeveloped wilds. No desert was too barren, no tribe of Indians too hostile, no climate too rigorous for their researches. Hunger, thirst, chilling snows and scorching sands seemed to give them new life and inspiration.

If one of them located a ledge of pure silver six feet thick, he would die in a week if he had to work it on his own account. Variety was the spice of their existence, the motive power of their lives. Neither disappointment nor the vicissitudes of climate could check the ardor of their enthusiasm.

Old prospectors were moon chasers, fearless men who could bear to be

alone. Although a rare breed today, a few still unroll a blanket at night, bake beans over a fire, and wearily plod the desert with pickax in hand.

—PHOTO COURTESY OF THE
NORTHEASTERN NEVADA MUSEUM, ELKO

on towards the white patches.

Luck was with him. The white patches did produce water enough to keep him alive. After a short rest, he unwrapped his bandanna and examined the chocolate-tinted quartz chunks. The nuggets of gold in them looked promising even to the bleary-eyed Breyfogle. If he could live to show this sample to an influential friend in the mining industry, his financial problems would be solved.

Without a canteen or even a hat to carry water, Breyfogle filled his shoes from the spring and headed out again. The next thing he could remember, when later trying to reconstruct his trek, was coming to a young mesquite tree. He ate some of its green

beans and drank a shoeful of water. After that, he blacked out.

Days later Breyfogle was found, struggling barefoot, along the old Spanish Trail at Las Vegas Spring on the east side of the Funerals, nearly dead from exposure, half crazed, but still clutching the bandanna filled with samples of quartz. A kindly couple traveling with a wagon train carried him to Austin. There, so the story goes, Breyfogle was rescued by an old friend and prominent mining man, Pony Duncan, and taken to Duncan's home in Salt Lake City.

After Breyfogle's ore samples were assayed in Austin, he had no trouble finding grubstakers. His chocolate quartz was the richest ore ever found in Death Valley.

Recovered from the near-fatal ordeal, Breyfogle returned to Austin to recruit a party of enterprising spirits to join him in retracing his route to the gold ledge. As the crow flies, it is more than two hundred miles from Austin to the twenty-square-mile region covering Stovepipe Wells, Boundary Canyon and Daylight Spring where Breyfogle believed he had found his rich ore.

The Austin party searched in vain. At Stovepipe Wells, bones of the slain Southerners were still strewn around the camp. Breyfogle's party also found mesquite trees and water holes, but none that led to the chocolate-colored quartz. When supplies ran low, the men begged Breyfogle to return with them to Austin, but the indomitable man had vowed to "come back a rich man or leave his bones in Death Valley." Again, he almost did.

Scorching sun, hunger and thirst were not the only perils he faced as, alone, he stumbled blindly through rockfalls, volcanic tufa and drifting sand for the second time. Two Paiutes who had been following his tracks south from Summit Springs in Boundary Canyon and along Nevada's dried-up Amargosa River finally overtook him at Stump Springs on the Spanish Trail. Approaching Breyfogle as he slept, the Paiutes beat him senseless and left him partially scalped. Again the man was rescued, this time by F. R. Granger's wagon train from Los Angeles. And again Breyfogle was returned to the care of his old friend Pony Duncan in Salt Lake City.

Breyfogle still hadn't given up. Among his other attempts to locate the lost ledge was a major one financed by the loyal Duncan who funded an elaborate camp in the heart of Death Valley at Furnace Creek Springs and staffed it with a knowledgeable crew of geologists. Under Breyfogle's direction, they more or less combed the desert, but the wasted man, once a pillar of muscle, now suffered spells of memory loss. After six weeks of aimless wandering around Death Valley, even Duncan lost faith and refused Breyfogle's plea to extend the search into the Amargosa Desert on the Nevada side of the Funerals.

Since Breyfogle's death in 1870 in Eureka, Nevada, more victims have succumbed in Death Valley while searching for his lost ledge than have been decapitated trying to find the Old Dutchman's mine in Arizona's Superstitions. Even the expression "Breyfogling around," meaning looking for something lost, has become common usage. Devastating heat, lack of water, and sidewinders were not the only early Death Valley perils. A maze of arroyos with endless trails took equal toll before the advent of air-conditioned autos and mapped highways. The barefoot Breyfogle suffered every one of them.

So goes the story of the legendary lost Breyfogle gold. Our next step in dissecting the anatomy of a treasure legend is to validate the facts. Possibilities are endless in contemplating Breyfogle's trail to gold, so we must waive them and concentrate purely on "givens."

It is a given that Breyfogle was rescued when half dead, but still clutching his sample of gold, on the Nevada side of the Funerals by a wagon train following the old Spanish Trail north. This trail veers through the southern end of Death Valley until it enters into the Amargosa Valley and turns directly north. The route connected San Bernardino in California with Salt Lake City, and was commonly used to transport freight and Mormon missionaries between the two cities.

It is a given that Breyfogle, himself, had wanted the Pony Duncan party to continue its probe into Nevada's Amargosa Valley, but after six weeks of unrewarding searches on the western side of the Funerals, the party had grown too skeptical of his guidance to pursue the matter further.

It is a given that Indians attacked the Southerners in their camp at Stovepipe Wells. The nearest Indian encampment to Stovepipe Wells was located on the eastern side of the Funerals at *Oasis Valley* in Nevada's

Amargosa Desert. Old trails radiating from the site are still evident. It is likely that Breyfogle, as delirious as he was, would have instinctively followed one of those trails looking for water.

It is a given that Breyfogle wandered deliriously for unknown days or nights follow-

Amargosa Desert on the Nevada side of the Funerals where Breyfogle was found, half dead, near the old Spanish Trail.

ing the attack at Stovepipe Wells. If he covered only ten miles a day, he could have been in the Amargosa Desert on the Nevada side of the Funerals in two days. Who knows upon which of those days he found his chocolate quartz with gold?

With the story told and its facts established, our third step in the anatomy of a treasure legend is to evaluate the prize. Fortunately, records are plentiful.

According to the inveterate prospector Shorty Harris, who saw a sample after Breyfogle's death, the chocolate quartz was the richest ore ever found in Death Valley.

Another credible source appraising Breyfogle's gold sample was J. Ross Browne, the most able reporter of western mining lore of his time. Browne had known Breyfogle in the 1850s when Breyfogle was employed as a tax collector in Alameda County, California, prior to moving to Nevada. They met again later in Austin, where Browne examined a sample of Breyfogle's ore. Browne also testified to its richness.

George Hearst, father of the notorious publisher and one of the most successful mining men of his day, secured a piece of Breyfogle's ore and was impressed enough to keep prospectors in the field searching for the vein for two winters.

Jake Gooding, a reliable, professional assayer, tested the ore that the half-dead Breyfogle brought into Austin after his calamitous trek across the desert. Gooding could hardly believe his eyes. The chocolate quartz proved fifty percent pure gold. Nothing to match it has been found in Death Valley since.

These burros are carrying the bodies of two prospectors who died of thirst in Death Valley.

Now that Breyfogle's story is told, its facts established and its prize evaluated, we must set about plotting a course. Countless prospectors since 1862, when Breyfogle came upon his golden ledge, have embroidered the legend. Today it is difficult to sift fact from fiction. In some accounts, the white patches of limestone that led Breyfogle to his first life-saving water source were "green spots" indicating plant life. Some have his trek into the desert initiating from Los Angeles instead of Austin. Even Breyfogle's first name, Charles, has become confused with that of a brother, Jake, who came looking for the ledge after Breyfogle's death. Our advantage in considering Breyfogle's adventure more than a century after the fact is that we can discount all of the hypothesis that failed.

Thus it appears doubtful to me that his gold-laden chocolate quartz lies within the Death Valley area confined to Stovepipe Wells, Daylight Springs and Boundary Canyon (in the Funerals on the California-Nevada border) where so many "Breyfoglers" have concentrated intensive searches. Prior to 1933, when awesome Death Valley acquired National Monument status, old-timers considered the thousands of adjacent miles in Nevada's Amargosa Desert as part of Death Valley. Limiting a search for Breyfogle's auspicious find to the perimeters of Death Valley Monument as we know it today, as some chroniclers have done, is unrealistic. When Breyfogle came upon his gold, he had been wandering for an unknown time. In jungle warfare a lost man in critical physical condition, with no sense of time, associates all areas encompassed in his wanderings, no matter how far afield, with the last clearly remembered landmark. This phenomenon may account for Breyfogle's tendency to focus his searches on the Death Valley side of the Funerals where his plight began.

Put imagination into play. Where would you have run in Breyfogle's place—in a strange country, in the dark of night? We know that he ended up east of the Funerals from the temporary camp at Stovepipe Wells where his companions were slain. There are only two feasible passes through the rugged Funeral Range.

The more distant one is southeast from Stovepipe Wells to Furnace Creek and then across the south end of the Funerals to what is now known as Death Valley Junction. Had Breyfogle escaped that way, he would have been traipsing barefoot through the torrid, earth-crackled valley floor now known as the Devil's Golf Course, 282 feet below sea level where blasting summer heat is known to soar as high as 137°F. To deliberately expose himself to that shadowless, flat stretch of desert would have been Breyfogle's death warrant.

My guess is that Breyfogle, while he still had his senses, escaped towards the protection of the Funeral Mountains silhouetted against the night sky directly east of Stovepipe Wells. This route through Daylight Pass follows an old Indian trail. It is now paved and leads to Beatty, Nevada. Averaging three miles an hour, the terrified man might have walked until dawn, covering as much as twenty-one miles and possibly already on the Nevada side of the Funerals when he hacked off his hunk of gold. That is why my own search for Breyfogle's gold, some November after the desert cools off,

will be concentrated in Nevada's Amargosa Desert rather than in Death Valley proper, so often associated with Breyfogle's find.

My plan of action is not original. It was while seeking Breyfogle's gold on the Funeral's eastern flank in 1904 that Shorty Harris picked up a glistening rock about the color and size of a bullfrog that launched the town of Rhyolite (now a ghost town) and initiated one of the most frenetic gold rushes Nevada has ever known. And it was while pursuing the Breyfogle legend in 1891 on the east edge of the Amargosa Desert that George Montgomery saw a quartz ledge so boldly studded with golden nuggets that he could break them off. He named his lode Chispa

The Funeral Mountains in which Breyfogle may have found his rich strike.

(Spanish for "nugget"). Other prospectors lured to the Amargosa Desert by his strike soon inaugurated a rival dig—the nearby Johnnie Mine. Both of these finds were believed to be the lost Breyfogle ledge, until experts proved that their ore didn't match Breyfogle's specimens. Mining in the Amargosa Desert has remained dormant since 1911.

Breyfogle's gold still awaits a modern seeker with the tenacity to accomplish what no other has managed in over a hundred years. Most of us are not interested in developing a mine, however. All we want to hold is one of those rocks packed with gold "like plums in a pudding."

So good luck, treasure hunters. Keep on the lookout for our dark green Range Rover. Maybe, Breyfogling along under a warm winter sun, we'll see you there!

THE ANATOMY OF A
TREASURE LEGEND

BIBLIOGRAPHY

Arnold, Oren. *Ghost Gold*. San Antonio, Texas: Naylor, 1971.

Bailey, Philip. *Golden Mirages*. New York: Macmillan Co., 1941.

Corle, Edwin. *Desert Country Duel*. New York: Sloan & Pearce, 1941.

Dimsdale, Thomas J. *Vigilantes of Montana*. Butte, Montana: McKee Printing Co., 1950.

Dobie, J. Frank. *Lost Mines and Buried Treasures*. New York: Grosset and Dunlap, 1930.

Drago, Harry Sinclair. *Lost Bonanzas*. New York: Dodd, Mead & Co., 1966.

Fisher, Vardin and Holmes. *Opal Gold Rushes and Mining Camps of the Early American West*. Caldwell, Idaho: Caxton Printers, 1968.

Florin, Lambert. *Ghost Towns of the West*. New York: Promontory Press, 1971.

Frost, Lawrence. *Custer Legends*. Ohio: Bowling Green University, 1981.

Gardner, Erle Stanley. *Hunting Lost Mines by Helicopter*. New York: Wm. Morrow, 1965.

Gibbs, James. *Shipwrecks of the Pacific Coast*. Portland, Oregon: Binford & Mort, 1957.

Henderson, Jeff. *The Treasure Legends of Castle Gap*. Texas: self-published, 1950.

Hoover, Rensch and Abeloe. *Historic Spots in California*. Stanford University Press, 1966.

Hult, Ruby E. *Lost Mines and Treasures*. Portland, Oregon: Binfords & Mort, 1960.

Lakes, Arthur. *Prospecting Gold and Silver in North America*. Scranton, Pennsylvania: International Textbooks, 1906.

Latham, John. *Famous Lost Mines of the Old West*. Texas: True Treasure Pub., 1971.

Lingenfelter, Richard. *Death Valley & The Amargosa*. University of California at Berkeley, 1986.

McAdams, Cliff. *Death Valley Past and Present*. Boulder, Colorado: Pruett, 1981.

McDonald, Douglas. *Nevada Lost Mines and Buried Treasures*. Las Vegas, Nevada: Nevada Publications, 1981.

Morgan, Dale. *The Great Salt Lake*. Albuquerque: University of New Mexico, 1947.

O'Connor, Richard. *The Cactus Throne*. New York: Putnam's Sons, 1971.

Pace, Dick. *Golden Gulch*. Virginia City: self-published, 1962.

Pepper, Choral. *Desert Lore of Southern California*. San Diego, California: Sunbelt Publishers, 1994.

Pepper, Choral, with Brad Williams. *The Mysterious West*. New York: World Pub., 1967.

Pepper, Choral, with Brad Williams. *Lost Legends of the West*. New York: Holt Rinehart and Winston, 1970, 1975.

Rieseberg, Harry. *Sunken Treasure Ships*. New York.: Frederick Fell, Inc., 1965.

Smith, Gene. *Maximilian and Carlota*. New York: Wm. Morrow, 1973.

Thompson, George. *Some Dreams Die*. Salt Lake City: self-published, 1982.

Thompson, George. *Faded Footprints*. Salt Lake City: self-published, 1991.

Thompson, George. *Lost Treasures*. Salt Lake City: self-published, 1992.

Wagner, Henry. *Spanish Voyages*. San Francisco: California Historical Society, 1929.

Weight, Harold and Lucile. *Tales and Trails of the Desert West*. Calico Press, 1953.

Wells, R. E. *Shipwreck Sites*. Canada: self-published, 1989.

ABOUT THE AUTHOR

Choral Pepper's name is closely associated with the literature and lore of the American West. In the sixties she owned and edited the former *Desert Magazine,* published in Palm Desert, California, and wrote four books now considered Southwestern classics.

After selling *Desert Magazine,* she moved to Los Angeles from where she covered the world for thirteen years to write a syndicated international travel column and frequent special assignments for the *Los Angeles Times, Christian Science Monitor,* and various travel publications.

Choral has written fifteen books, her most recent prior to *Treasure Legends of the West* being *Desert Lore of Southern California* and *Walks in Oscar Wilde's London.*

She lives summers in Salt Lake City, Utah, and winters in Coronado, California, with her husband Denis Thompson.